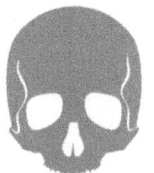

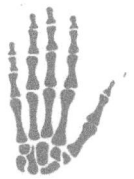

The FORGOTTEN PAST II

Another Eclectic Collection of Little-Known Stories from the Annals of History

Andrew Vinken

Copyright © 2024 Andrew Vinken

The moral right of the author has been asserted.

Apart from any fair dealing for the purposes of research or private study, or criticism or review, as permitted under the Copyright, Designs and Patents Act 1988, this publication may only be reproduced, stored or transmitted, in any form or by any means, with the prior permission in writing of the publishers, or in the case of reprographic reproduction in accordance with the terms of licences issued by the Copyright Licensing Agency. Enquiries concerning reproduction outside those terms should be sent to the publishers

Matador
Unit E2 Airfield Business Park,
Harrison Road, Market Harborough,
Leicestershire. LE16 7UL
Tel: 0116 279 2299
Email: books@troubador.co.uk
Web: www.troubador.co.uk/matador
Twitter: @matadorbooks

ISBN 978 1 80514 341 3

British Library Cataloguing in Publication Data.
A catalogue record for this book is available from the British Library.

Printed and bound by CPI Group (UK) Ltd, Croydon, CR0 4YY
Typeset in 11pt Aldine401 by Troubador Publishing Ltd, Leicester, UK

Matador is an imprint of Troubador Publishing Ltd

Contents

Introduction xi

1. The Comte de Saint-Germain: The Immortal Count? 1
2. Bear Necessities 6
3. The Remarkable Life and Times of Charles Herbert Lightoller 11
4. The Strange Double Life of Emilie Sagee 17
5. The Remarkable Life of Sir Arthur Conan Doyle 21
6. The Enigmatic DB Cooper 26
7. The Disappearance of Frederick Valentich 32
8. God's Own Diver 37
9. The Ghost Who Solved His Own Murder? 42
10. The Extendable Clarence Willard 47
11. Titanic Twice? 51

12.	Colonel Blood and the Crown Jewels Heist	55
13.	The Electrifying Andrew Crosse	61
14.	Hell on Earth	66
15.	The Curse of Flight 191	71
16.	The Strange Case of the Actress and the Skeleton	76
17.	The Real Ebeneezer Scrooge	80
18.	Tamam Shud – The Somerton Man Mystery	84
19.	A Degree of Error	91
20.	Abandoned Cyprus	95
21.	Hooray Henry	101
22.	The Mysterious Death of Alfred Loewenstein	105
23.	Korla Pandit – The Indian Music Maestro?	110
24.	The Many Lives of Stanley Jacob Weinberg	114
25.	Bittersweet Kiss	119
26.	A Strange Romance	123
27.	The Men From Nowhere	128
28.	The Mysterious Death of Elisa Lam at the Cecil Hotel	133
29.	Porky Bickar and the Mount Edgecumbe Eruption	137
30.	The Science of Lazarus	142
31.	The Whimsical Horace de Vere Cole	147
32.	Jacob Miller's Tough Nut	152
33.	The Sin-Eaters	158
34.	The Amazing Victorian Machine of Death	163
35.	The Resurrection of George Hayward	167

36.	The Artful Dexter?	172
37.	The Disappearance of Star Dust	177
38.	The Remarkable Survival of Edward Oxford	182
39.	And the Band Played On	187
	Appendix 1: Images	192
	Appendix 2: Sources	200

Introduction

A learned academic once told me to think of history as being like a country to which you cannot go. I remember thinking that was an odd way to look at it, as clearly one can visit historical places that have survived the passage of time. However, upon reflection, I think he was merely trying to say, in his roundabout way, that you cannot travel back in time to a bygone era. The Tower of London, for example, is a fascinating place to visit, but you cannot go back and experience the traumatic events that have played out there down the centuries.

And while time travel remains elusive to us, who has not, at one time or another, daydreamed about the possibility of being able to go back in time to witness dramatic historical occurrences? The Battle of Thermopylae or the surrender of Napoleon Bonaparte are just a couple of examples that spring to mind. However, as I mentioned in my introduction to the first volume of *The Forgotten Past*, my interest lies not in the earth-shattering, game-changing events of the past, but in the fascinating tales that did not change the world and, as a consequence of which, have been largely forgotten.

Since the publication of *The Forgotten Past* in 2019, I have spent many happy hours compiling a new collection of eclectic tales of little-known stories from times gone by. And while we may not be able to travel back and bear personal witness to these events, I nevertheless hope that you will join me for another romp through the backwaters of history. I hope you enjoy the book.

Andrew Vinken
Buckinghamshire, England
September 2023

ONE

THE COMTE DE SAINT-GERMAIN: THE IMMORTAL COUNT?

Surely no man has ever drawn breath whose life was shrouded in more mystery than the individual who went, or goes, by the name of the Comte de Saint-Germain. The most we can really say about him is that he actually existed, but of more than that we cannot be certain. Let's start at the beginning, or as close as we can get to the beginning. His year of birth is given alternatively as 1691 or 1712, although he was also said to have been a guest at the wedding at Cana where Jesus famously turned water into wine, and he was also reported to have attended an ecclesiastical assembly known as the First Council of Nicaea in 325CE. You're probably wondering what on earth I am talking about – and with much justification. Even if he was born in 1691, he would still have been well over a millennium too young to have attended either of the events in question.

An account of a purported conversation between the comte and one Countess von Georgy adds even further to the enigma, and indicates that his year of birth must have been considerably earlier than either of the years suggested above. In 1760, the countess was an elderly lady and was attending a soirée in Paris given by Madame de Pompadour, mistress of King Louis XV of France. Upon being introduced to the comte, the countess recalled having met him fifty years earlier in Venice in 1710, but as he didn't appear to have aged in half a century, she simply made the assumption that it must have been the current Comte's father that she had encountered all those years earlier. The conversation between the two is reported to have proceeded as follows:

"No, Madame," replied the comte, "but I myself was living in Venice at the end of the last and the beginning of this century; I had the honour to pay you court then."

The Comte de Saint-Germain.

"Forgive me, but that is impossible!" replied the astonished countess. "The Comte de Saint-Germain I knew in those days was at least forty-five years old. And you, at the outside, are that age at present."

"Madame, I am very old," he responded.

"But then you must be nearly one hundred years old," said the flabbergasted aristocrat.

"That is not impossible," said the comte, before going on to recall details of their previous encounter that eventually convinced her that he really was the same man she had met in Venice fifty years earlier.

So what is the explanation for the man's incredible longevity? Apparently, the Comte de Saint-Germain was an expert in the art of alchemy. Not only was he able to turn base metals into gold, but he also discovered an elixir that would impart immortality to those who consumed it. Having quaffed a quantity of it himself, presumably when aged about forty-five, he was thus destined to live forever.

Being of such great age, he exuded the wisdom and grace of enormous experience and displayed considerable artistic ability. The comte travelled extensively throughout Europe and charmed his way into the company of the continent's royalty and upper classes. He was wined and dined by the upper echelons of society, but was never seen to eat, instead drinking only, what appeared to be, red wine.

The French Enlightenment philosopher Voltaire, a contemporary of the comte, said of him: "a man who never dies, and who knows everything". Upon meeting the comte in 1760, the famous Italian author Casanova commented: "This extraordinary man… would say in an easy, assured manner that he was three hundred years old, that he knew the secret of the Universal Medicine, that he possessed a mastery over nature, that he could melt diamonds… all this, he said, was mere trifle to him."

So, what became of the old Comte? Well, the simple answer is we don't know. According to one account, he travelled to Hamburg in modern-day Germany in 1779, where he became acquainted with Prince Charles of Hesse-Kassel, who considered him to be 'one of the greatest philosophers who ever lived'. There he stayed, as a guest of the prince at his castle at Eckernförde, where, as this version of events goes, he died on 27th February 1784. However, that is far from the end of the story of this remarkable individual. In 1785, he was reportedly seen in the company of Anton Mesmer, the pioneering hypnotist, who, it is claimed, learned his hypnotic techniques from the comte. Also, Freemasonry records indicate that the Comte de Saint-Germain was chosen as their representative for a convention in 1785. He popped up again in 1789, 1815, 1820 and 1821.

Between 1880 and 1900, it was claimed that he was involved with the Theosophical Society and that he was working towards the spiritual development of the West. In 1897, the French opera singer Emma Calve autographed a portrait of herself and dedicated it to the Comte. More recently, a man turned up in Paris in 1972 claiming to be the Comte de Saint-Germain, although he was now living under the name Richard Chanfray. Chanfray later took his own life in Saint Tropez in 1983, although it has been alleged that no body was discovered, just a suicide note.

Richard Chanfray.

Most recently of all, it has been noted that American actor, comedian, and impressionist Kevin Pollak bears a striking resemblance to portraits of the Comte. When this was pointed out to him, he happily confirmed that he was indeed the immortal Comte de Saint-Germain. However, do bear in mind that Kevin is a comedian.

The Comte de Saint-Germain

was undoubtedly a man of great charm and intellect, who earned a reputation in his own lifetime for his extraordinary abilities. That reputation, however, seems to have grown into the stuff of fanciful legend over the intervening years. Or did he really discover the elixir of eternal life? If so, we may not have heard the last of the Comte de Saint-Germain.

TWO

BEAR NECESSITIES

Next time your boss bawls you out for something that really wasn't your fault, or your computer refuses all attempts to cooperate despite your best endeavours, spare a thought for Hugh Glass, a man who surely had one of the worst days at work of all time!

Glass was born around 1783 in Scranton, Pennsylvania, in the United States, to parents who had emigrated from Ireland. He died in 1833, after being attacked by a party of Arikara warriors, a Native American tribe from North Dakota. This is about as much as can be said about Hugh with any real certainty, as he left no personal written account of his life, but one particular adventure that he undertook has become the stuff of legend. As legends tend to ripen in the retelling, what follows needs to be taken with a pinch of salt, although as tales of his daring escapades first appeared in print in 1825, during his own lifetime, one can surmise that his extraordinary story is largely based in fact.

By the 1820s, Glass was working as a fur trapper, explorer and guide in an area now known as Montana, and North and South Dakota. In 1822, the Rocky Mountain Fur Company, founded by General William Henry Ashley, placed an advertisement in the *Missouri Gazette and Public Advertiser*, inviting men to join them on a fur-trading venture that would entail navigating the Missouri, Grand and Yellowstone Rivers. Hugh responded to the advert and was duly hired. The party departed in the spring of 1823.

On 2nd June, the expedition was attacked by Arikara warriors and several members were killed. Glass was wounded, having been shot in the leg. Undeterred, the depleted company pressed on and, despite his injury, Hugh was able to keep up with the group. By August, they had reached the forks of the Grand River in present-day Perkins County, South Dakota.

It was at this point that Hugh Glass experienced a bad day at work. While out hunting for game, he came upon a grizzly bear with two cubs. Alarmed by his presence, the bear attacked. Glass had no time to pull out his rifle and so had only his hunting knife with which to defend himself. Hearing the commotion, the rest of the hunting party ran to his aid. By the time they got there, it was all over. Hugh was in a bad way. The teeth and claws of the bear had caused terrible injuries; he had a broken leg, his ribs were visible through severe lacerations, and air could be seen bubbling through blood in a deep throat wound. However, to the astonishment of all present, next to him lay the body of the bear. Amazingly, Hugh Glass had fought an adult grizzly bear and won – just!

A Contemporary Illustration of the Attack – Unknown.

Despite his heroic effort, Hugh's injuries were so extreme that he was not expected to survive. Two volunteers, called Fitzpatrick and Bridges, agreed to stay with Glass until he succumbed to his injuries, at which point they were to bury him and subsequently rejoin the main group. While waiting for Hugh to die, they began digging his grave.

What happened next cannot be verified, but when Fitzpatrick and Bridges caught up with the main party, they confirmed that Glass had died. However, they claimed that they had been interrupted by an Arikara warrior attack and had been forced to flee before they could inter him. They had in their possession his knife, rifle and some other items of his equipment.

Hugh Glass was not dead, however, merely comatose. When he eventually regained consciousness, he found himself to be lying next to a freshly dug hole, completely alone and without weapons or equipment. Aware that Fort Kiowa, the nearest settlement, was some 200 miles away, Hugh nevertheless determined that the only course of action available to him was to head in the direction of the fort, which was located on the Missouri River.

Despite incredible pain, festering wounds and severe blood loss, he set his own leg and tied a stick to it to act as a splint. Wrapping himself in the hide of the deceased bear, which his companions had laid over him to keep him warm, he began to crawl his way towards civilisation. Realising that his injuries were likely to become gangrenous, he allowed maggots to eat the dead flesh of his wounds, successfully preventing infection from spreading around his body and killing him. Glass sustained himself by eating berries and rattlesnakes, the latter of which he killed with rocks. On one occasion, he was even able to feast on a bison calf, after having frightened off the wolves who had just killed it.

Well over a month after he had set off, Hugh finally reached the Missouri River, where he fashioned a raft out of logs and floated downriver. In October 1823, Glass finally arrived at Fort Kiowa, some eight weeks after being attacked by the bear – surely one of the most remarkable cases of survival through sheer will and determination.

Unsurprisingly, it took Hugh a number of years to recuperate from his injuries, but he was nonetheless eventually able to resume his career as a guide and fur trapper. He also determined to track down the two men who had left him for dead, in order to seek retribution for them having abandoned him in such dire circumstances.

However, he found that Fitzgerald had since joined the army and so he was unable to take revenge against him, as to do so would have meant harming a soldier of the United States Army – a crime that would have resulted in severe punishment. He did, however, manage to recover the rifle Fitzgerald had stolen from him. Bridger, it turned out, was still with the

Hugh Glass Monument – John Lopez.

Rocky Mountain Fur Company and soon found himself in the uncomfortable position of being confronted by his abandoned charge. Owing to his comparative youth, however, Glass chose to forgive him and instead of reducing General Ashley's personnel by one, Hugh himself re-enlisted with the company.

A monument to Hugh Glass can be found on the southern shore of Shadehill Reservoir in Perkins County, South Dakota, close to the spot on which he took on the grizzly bear and won.

THREE

THE REMARKABLE LIFE AND TIMES OF CHARLES HERBERT LIGHTOLLER

If you are at all familiar with the name Charles Lightoller, it is probably through his association with the RMS *Titanic*, which sank in the North Atlantic on her maiden voyage on 15th April 1912, with the loss of more than 1,500 lives, following a collision with an iceberg. However, the fact that he is remembered today solely as a crew member of the ill-fated liner does him a major disservice. Charles Herbert Lightoller was born on 30th March 1874 in Chorley, Lancashire, England to Sarah and Fred Lightoller. Sadly, Sarah died soon after giving birth and Fred abandoned his young son, seeking a new life for himself in New Zealand.

At the age of thirteen, Charles began a seafaring apprenticeship that would last four years. Unfortunately for the young mariner, it was certainly not plain sailing. On only his second voyage, the ship on which he was serving, the *Holt Hill*, was damaged in a storm and was forced to seek shelter at Rio de Janeiro, which just happened to be in the middle of a revolution and a smallpox epidemic at the time. Nevertheless, repairs were made and the ship was able to continue on with its voyage – that was until 13th November 1889, when another storm caused the ship to run aground on an uninhabited island in the Indian Ocean. The crew were eventually rescued and taken to Adelaide, Australia, where Lightoller managed to join the crew of a clipper called *The Duke of Abercorn*, which was sailing for England.

While serving as third mate on a windjammer called *Knight of St. Michael*, Charles found himself embroiled in another nautical nightmare, when the cargo of coal caught fire. On this occasion, however, the young seaman distinguished himself by successfully extinguishing the blaze and therefore saving the ship. For his endeavours, he was rewarded with a promotion to second mate. In 1895, at the age of twenty-one, Lightoller switched from sail to steam and joined the African Royal Mail Service, steaming up and down the West African coast. However, after three years, Charles contracted a severe bout of malaria, which almost cost him his life.

Charles Lightoller (circa 1910).

Following his recovery, Lightoller decided to pursue a different career path. In 1898, he headed for the Yukon to prospect for gold, in what became known as the Klondike Gold Rush. Unfortunately, he didn't strike it rich and so headed instead for Alberta, Canada, where he worked for a time as a cowboy, before eventually working his passage home aboard a cattle boat, arriving back in England, penniless, in 1899.

In January of 1900, Charles elected to resume his maritime career and joined the White Star Line as fourth officer on the SS *Medic*. It was while serving aboard the *Medic*, and while moored in Sydney Harbour, Australia that an incident occurred that suggested Lightoller possessed a slightly eccentric sense of humour. Noting the concern of locals as to the potential outcome of the Boer War, which was raging in far-off South Africa at the time, Charles decided to play a trick on the residents of Sydney. Just after midnight on Saturday 6th October 1900, Lightoller and two shipmates took a rowing boat and rowed out to Fort Denison in the harbour. There, they hoisted a Boer flag and loaded a cannon with 14 pounds of blasting powder and a long fuse; the idea being to fool the good citizens of the city into thinking they were being attacked by a Boer raiding party. At 1am, the cannon went off, and the ensuing blast was so loud that windows were blown out and startled residents leapt from their beds. When the Boer flag was spotted, panic ensued.

Thanks to the long fuse, Charles and his accomplices had made good their escape by the time of the explosion and the perpetrators of the stunt were never apprehended. Burdened by guilt over the incident, however, Lightoller admitted his involvement to the line's marine superintendent once back in England. Fortunately, instead of disciplining him, the officer found the whole thing highly amusing and simply told him to get on with his duties.

At the beginning of April 1912, Charles Lightoller was appointed to the position of Second Officer aboard the RMS *Titanic* – a commission that would seal his place in history. On the night of 14th April, Charles had already retired to bed when he felt *'a sudden vibrating jar run through the ship'*. Being told that they had struck an iceberg, Lightoller got dressed and made his way up onto the deck of the stricken vessel. His initial confidence that the ship would not sink soon evaporated and Charles immediately began the task of loading passengers into lifeboats. His actions in this regard have subsequently met with some criticism. He interpreted the order of 'women and children first' to mean 'women and children only', meaning some lifeboats were launched with spare capacity remaining. Lightoller even refused to allow the millionaire businessman John Jacob Astor to accompany his wife into a lifeboat. Astor subsequently drowned.

As it became clear the ship was about to go under, Lightoller and his fellow officers shook hands and said goodbye to one another. With nothing more to be done

A Depiction of the Titanic Disaster – Willy Stöwer.

aboard the crippled liner, Charles dived off of the roof of the officers' quarters into the frigid waters of the North Atlantic. He somehow managed to avoid being dragged under by the colossal suction forces generated by the sinking leviathan and was able to swim to an upturned lifeboat, which he clung to until rescued. Charles Lightoller thus became the most senior officer to survive the *Titanic* disaster.

Having lived through such a traumatic ordeal, one might think that that would have signalled the end of Charles' life on the ocean waves – but not so. There were still more tales of derring-do to come from our intrepid hero. During World War I, Lightoller enlisted in the Royal Navy and was given the command of a torpedo boat. He served with distinction, on one occasion even sinking a German submarine. By the end of hostilities, he had been decorated on two occasions and emerged with the rank of naval commander.

After the war, Charles retired and bought his own boat named *Sundowner*, and together with his Australian wife, Sylvia, spent many happy years cruising around northern Europe. Yes, that's right, despite antagonising almost the entire population of Sydney, he actually married a girl – from Sydney! I wonder if he ever confessed his guilt to his in-laws!

Even in retirement, however, the world had not seen the last of Charles Lightoller. In 1940, after the outbreak of World War II, the British Army, along with troops from France and Belgium, found themselves trapped on the beaches of Dunkirk, France, with the German army approaching from land on one side and the English Channel on the other.

Desperate times call for desperate measures, and

Charles' Boat, Sundowner.

the owners of boats in the south of England were informed that their vessels were needed to rescue the troops stranded on the French beaches. The retired commander immediately sprang into action, determining to take the *Sundowner* to France himself. And so it was that on 27th May 1940, sixty-six-year-old Charles Lightoller, together with his son, Roger, and a sea scout named Gerald Ashcroft, set sail for Dunkirk. Despite being under aerial attack from German fighter aircraft, they managed to cram an astonishing 260 men on board the *Sundowner* and all were successfully evacuated back to England. On watching the disembarkation, one astounded officer commented to Charles, "My God, mate! Where did you put 'em all?"

Charles Herbert Lightoller DSC & Bar, RD died of heart failure on 8th December 1952 at the age of seventy-eight. His ashes were scattered at the Commonwealth 'Garden of Remembrance' at Mortlake Crematorium, Surrey, next to the River Thames. A life well lived, I think.

FOUR

THE STRANGE DOUBLE LIFE OF EMILIE SAGEE

Emilie Sagee was a teacher. In fact, she was two teachers. No, she didn't take the exam twice, it's just that she was, well, plural. Emilie One was born in Dijon, France in 1813 and her story comes to us from a book called *Footfalls on the Boundary of Another World* by Robert Dale Owen, published in 1860. According to Dale Owen, he learned of the strange story of Emilie Sagee from Julie von Guldenstubbe, the daughter of Baron von Guldenstubbe, who had been a pupil at a boarding school called Pensionat von Neuwelcke in present-day Latvia in 1845. It was in this year that Julie became acquainted with Emilie, who had recently joined the school in a teaching capacity.

By all accounts, the thirty-two-year-old teacher was bright, engaging and popular with pupils and colleagues alike. It was surprising, therefore, that in the sixteen years that she had been in employment,

Emilie had worked at eighteen different teaching establishments. However, the reason for her rapid turnover of employers did not take long to present itself. While teaching a class of seventeen girls, Emilie had her back to the students, writing on the blackboard when, to the utter consternation of her attentive charges, a duplicate Emilie suddenly appeared next to the teacher, imitating her movements, minus the chalk stick the real Emilie was using to write with.

It appeared that Emilie Sagee had a doppelganger! A doppelganger is defined as 'a ghostly double or counterpart of a living person', and in many cultures it is considered a bad omen to encounter one's own doppelganger. Fortunately, in this particular case, it seems that Emilie could never see her own double, although apparently everyone else could. The best witnessed incident of her being seen in two places at once occurred one day when she was gardening, while a large class of forty-two girls were being given sewing lessons. When the teacher giving the class needed to leave the room for a few minutes, Emilie walked in and sat down, as if taking over supervision in the needlework teacher's absence. The only trouble was that the pupils soon realised that she was also still outside gardening. Terrifying as the apparition of Emilie Two must have been, a few girls courageously approached the spectre and one even touched it, noting that her hand passed through it with only a minimal cobweb-like resistance.

Most commonly, however, Emilie Two would appear next to Emilie One, imitating her movements, such as when eating or teaching her class. On one occasion, Emilie was helping a pupil with a costume she wanted to wear to an event. When the student glanced down to see how Emilie was getting on with the adjustments, she was stunned to find two Emilies working on the dress. She promptly passed out from shock.

Apparently, poor Emilie had no explanation for her doppelganger. She never saw it herself and had no control over it. People noted that whenever her twin put in an appearance, the real Emilie looked pale and lethargic. As soon as the apparition vanished, however, she immediately returned to normal. It seemed as though her double needed to sap her energy in order to be able to manifest itself.

Unfortunately for her, students found the ghostly twin so upsetting that many parents started to remove their children from the school. As a consequence, the principal had little option but to terminate Emilie's contract of employment. Thus ended Emilie's nineteenth assignment in less than seventeen years. Sadly, as the source of story, Julie von Guldenstubbe thereafter had no further contact with her former teacher, we have no idea of what became of Emilie Sagee and her unwanted sidekick.

So, what are we to make of this strange and perplexing tale? The easiest explanation is simply that it isn't true and was a work of fiction made up by either Julie von Guldenstubbe or Robert Dale Owen. Owing to the passage of almost two hundred years, we are unlikely to ever know for certain, one way or the other.

However, history does seem to be littered with sober-minded individuals who claim to have encountered doppelgangers. A duplicate of Catherine the Great, Empress of Russia from 1762 to 1796, was seen by numerous people entering her throne room, even though the real Catherine was lying in bed at the time. Elizabeth I, Queen of England from 1558 to 1603, discovered a corpse-like version of herself, apparently lying in state, upon entering her chambers. A few days later, the queen was dead. Poet Percy Shelley encountered his doppelganger on two occasions and during one encounter, it even spoke to him, asking, "How long do you mean to be content?" But perhaps the most notorious encounter with a spectral double occurred to Abraham Lincoln, who, when glancing at a mirror saw two images of himself: the normal one and a paler more deathly reflection. He told his wife who thought it a bad omen. We all know what happened next.

If you are inclined to believe any of this at all, an intriguing possibility as to what may have been occurring comes to us from Emilie herself, who is reported to have said that during the incident that occurred while she was gardening, she was suddenly overcome with an urge to go inside the classroom to supervise the children. Could her mere desire to be in another place have been sufficient to project an image of herself to that very place? Although, as Emilie claimed to have no control over her spectral double, this seems unlikely.

Alternatively, might quantum physics offer an explanation to the doppelganger phenomenon? Quantum physics, or quantum mechanics as it is sometimes referred, is the study of nature at atomic and subatomic levels, and suggests the possibility of multiple dimensions. Might a version of Emilie from a parallel universe have occasionally transgressed the dimensional veil and unwittingly given those shocked students a glimpse of herself in another existence?

FIVE

THE REMARKABLE LIFE OF SIR ARTHUR CONAN DOYLE

If you are at all familiar with the name of Sir Arthur Conan Doyle, it is probably as the writer and creator of the fictional detective Sherlock Holmes. You may even be aware that he had a strong interest in spiritualism and, more generally, in all things paranormal. Being a prolific bestselling author, as well as an avid seeker of the spooky stuff, should have kept him fairly busy, you would be forgiven for thinking – but not a bit of it. It transpires that Sir Arthur was a man of varied talents, who led a life of astonishing variety.

However, let us firstly clear up a popular misconception. Arthur Ignatius Conan Doyle was born in Edinburgh, Scotland on 22nd May 1859. However, his baptism entry gives 'Arthur Ignatius Conan' as his given names and 'Doyle' as his surname. It seems that at some point, presumably to make himself sound more impressive, he started to use Conan Doyle as a compound surname. However, he actually started life as plain old Arthur Doyle.

Unfortunately, life did not start well for young Arthur. Owing to his father's increasing alcoholism, the family was temporarily split up in 1864, before reuniting three years later, but they ended up residing in a squalid tenement flat. Fortunately, however, Doyle had wealthy uncles who took the decision to pay for his education, so Arthur was sent firstly to a Jesuit preparatory school in Lancashire, England, followed by a Jesuit school in Feldkirch, Austria, in order to perfect his German, as well broadening his academic horizons.

After finishing school, Doyle elected to study medicine and botany, graduating with Bachelor of Medicine and Master of Surgery degrees from the University of Edinburgh in 1881. His first professional appointments were maritime. He firstly served as ship's doctor on a Greenland whaler, followed by a post of ship's surgeon on the SS *Mayumba* during a voyage to the West African coast. Thereafter, he worked in England as a general practitioner at medical practices in Plymouth and Portsmouth, before deciding to specialise as an ophthalmologist (eye doctor, in case you were wondering) and setting up his own practice in London.

It was around this time that Doyle also began his literary career, which was both wide-ranging and prolific, although he is best remembered as the creator of the fictional detective Sherlock Holmes, whom he based on one of his university tutors, Joseph Bell. However, as it is his literary achievements for which he is commemorated today, I will instead concentrate on other aspects of this fascinating man's life.

Let us first take a look at the sporting career of Arthur Ignatius Conan Doyle. While living and practising medicine in Portsmouth, Doyle was also goalkeeper for Portsmouth Association Football Club (a soccer team, to our American friends). He was also a keen, and reasonably talented, cricketer. Between 1899 and 1907, he played ten first-class matches for the Marylebone Cricket Club (MCC). His highest innings score came in 1902, when he scored forty-three. He also occasionally bowled and although he only took one first-class wicket, it was some wicket. He bowled out none other than W.G Grace, the greatest cricketer of his generation and considered by many as one of the greatest of all time.

He was also keen on bodybuilding and in 1901 he was one of three judges at the world's first major bodybuilding competition held at the Royal Albert Hall in London. As if all that wasn't enough, Arthur was also an amateur boxer and, in 1909, he was invited to referee the world heavyweight championship fight between James Jeffries and Jack Johnson in Reno, Nevada, USA. Unfortunately, his pre-existing commitments meant he was unable to accept the invitation. You don't say! He

Sir Arthur Conan Doyle in 1914.

also enjoyed playing golf and was elected captain of the Crowborough Beacon Golf Club in Sussex, England for the year 1910. He entered the English amateur billiards championship in 1913. He also somehow found time to learn to ski and ice skate.

During the Boer War (1899–1902), Doyle volunteered for active service, but at forty was considered too old, so he instead served as a volunteer doctor at a field hospital in Bloemfontein, South Africa. It was for his service to his country that on 24th October 1902, he was knighted by King Edward VII at Buckingham Palace. He twice stood for parliament, in 1900 and again in 1906, but despite receiving a respectable share of the vote, he was not successful on either occasion. He served as Deputy Lieutenant of Surrey from 1902.

A fervent advocate of justice, Doyle became involved in two closed criminal cases. His investigations led to the exoneration of two men who had been wrongly accused and convicted of crimes. The first, in 1906, concerned a lawyer named George Edalji, who had been convicted of animal mutilation. The conviction had been upheld despite the fact that the mutilations continued even after Edalji had been jailed. Doyle's work on the case was partly responsible for the establishment of the Court of Criminal Appeal in 1907. The second case involved a man named Oscar Slater, who had been convicted of bludgeoning an eighty-two-year-old woman in Glasgow. Inconsistencies in the prosecution's case led Doyle to believe he was not guilty and, in 1928, his appeal against conviction was successful.

So, there we have it. Medical practitioner, botanist, footballer, cricketer, boxer, golfer, war veteran, prospective parliamentarian, paranormal investigator and righter of wrongs. Given everything he had to keep him occupied, it's a wonder that Sherlock Holmes ever saw the light of day.

On 7th July 1930, Sir Arthur Conan Doyle was discovered clutching his chest in the hall of Windlesham Manor, his home in Crowborough, East Sussex, England. He died of a heart attack shortly thereafter at the age of seventy-one. His last words, spoken to his wife, were: "You are wonderful." Owing to his spiritualist ideology, it was not thought appropriate to lay him to rest in consecrated ground and, as a consequence, he was initially buried in the rose garden at Windlesham Manor. However, following the death of his wife, he was reinterred next to her in the churchyard of All Saints' Church, Minstead in the New Forest, Hampshire, England. The epitaph on his gravestone reads: 'Steel True, Blade Straight, Arthur Conan Doyle, Knight, Patriot, Physician & Man Of Letters'. That was putting it mildly.

SIX

THE ENIGMATIC DB COOPER

On 24th November 1971, a man in his mid-forties, wearing a suit and carrying a briefcase, calling himself Dan Cooper, purchased a one-way ticket with cash from the Northwest Orient Airlines flight counter at Portland International Airport for flight 305 – a short thirty-minute hop to Seattle. He boarded the aircraft, a Boeing 727-100, settled himself into seat 18C and ordered a bourbon and soda. Shortly after take-off at 2.50pm PST, the man handed a note to Florence Schaffner, the flight attendant seated nearest to him at the rear of the aircraft. The note informed her that he had a bomb in his briefcase. Cooper told Schaffner to sit beside him and proceeded to explain his demands. He required $200,000 in 'negotiable American currency', four parachutes and a fuel truck to be on standby at Seattle in order to refuel the aircraft upon arrival. Calmly, Schaffner asked to see the bomb. Dan obligingly opened the briefcase just wide enough to reveal eight red cylinders, four on top of four, attached to wires coated with red insulation, and a large cylindrical battery. Schaffner informed the flight crew in the cockpit of Cooper's demands. When she returned, she noticed that the hijacker had donned a pair of dark sunglasses.

Pilot William A Scott relayed the information to air traffic control, who in turn notified local and federal authorities. Donald Nyrop, President of Northwest Orient Airlines, promptly authorised payment of the ransom and directed all employees to cooperate fully with the hijacker. The aircraft flew in a holding pattern over Puget Sound for approximately two hours to allow sufficient time for police and the FBI to assemble the money and parachutes. Another of the flight attendants, Tina Mucklow, recalled Cooper as being calm and polite. She said he also appeared to be familiar with the local terrain from the air. Meanwhile, FBI agents collected the ransom money from several local banks in 10,000 unmarked twenty-dollar bills, although the serial numbers were recorded. During this time, police also obtained the parachutes from a local skydiving school.

Once in place, Cooper was advised that everything had been arranged as instructed and, at 5.39pm, the aircraft landed at Seattle-Tacoma Airport. Al Lee, the airline's Seattle operations manager, cautiously approached the aircraft and handed a rucksack containing the cash and the parachutes to Mucklow via the rear stairs. Once the delivery had been completed, Cooper allowed all passengers, plus Schaffner and the senior flight attendant, Alice Hancock, to leave the plane.

While the aircraft was being refuelled and prepared for take-off, Dan informed the flight crew that they were to fly the plane to Mexico City, but with very specific instructions as to the aircraft's configuration. They were to fly at the minimum airspeed possible without stalling the aircraft, which was about 185kmh or 115mph and at a maximum altitude of 10,000ft or 3000m. He also instructed that the landing gear remain deployed throughout, that the wing flaps be lowered fifteen degrees, and the cabin should remain unpressurised. Realising that this flight configuration would limit the range of the aircraft to approximately 1000 miles or 1600 kilometres, co-pilot William J Rataczak explained to Cooper that they would be unable to reach Mexico City without a second refuelling stop. The crew discussed the options with Cooper and agreed on Reno, Nevada.

At around 7.40pm, the aircraft took off, heading for Reno. An unusual design feature of the Boeing 727 was that it had its own integral staircase at the rear of the aircraft, via which passengers boarded and alighted. Once airborne, Cooper instructed Mucklow to join the flight crew in the cockpit and to remain there with the door closed. At approximately 8pm, a warning light lit up in the cockpit indicating that the rear staircase had been deployed into the lowered position and a change in

Artist's Impression of DB Cooper.

air pressure soon confirmed that this was, in fact, the case. About thirteen minutes later, an upwards motion was felt in the tail section, consistent with someone jumping off the staircase and causing it to recoil upwards, which required corrective action on the part of the pilots. When the aircraft landed at Reno Airport at around 10.15pm, the staircase remained in the lowered position. The Boeing 727 was surrounded by FBI agents, state troopers, sheriff's deputies and Reno police, as it had not yet been established whether the hijacker remained aboard. However, an armed search soon revealed that Dan Cooper was no longer on board the aircraft. Somewhere en route to Reno, he had bailed out with $200,000 in cash. But where? $200,000 in 1971 is equivalent to approximately $1,300,000 in 2020.

Although the name Dan Cooper was almost certainly an alias, all lines of enquiry were pursued. One suspect who was quickly ruled out was an individual known to police as DB Cooper. However, due to a misunderstanding between police and journalists, the hijacker was referred to in the media as going by the name of DB Cooper. Perhaps because this name is more enigmatic than plain old Dan Cooper, the moniker stuck – and despite the individual in question never using the initials, he is known today as DB Cooper.

Despite an extensive manhunt and a protracted FBI investigation, the man who hijacked flight 305 has never been located or identified. Many theories and suspects have been

Boeing 727 With Lowered Rear Staircase.

investigated with no firm leads. Could he have even survived the descent? It was cold and raining heavily and he was wearing just a business suit. Opinion is divided on this one, although no remains have ever been found. Only two pieces of evidence were ever discovered on the ground and they tend to suggest that he did, indeed, survive the jump.

In November 1978, a placard printed with instructions for lowering the rear stairs of a Boeing 727 was found by a deer hunter within Flight 305's basic flight path. And on 10th February 1980, eight-year-old Brian Ingram was playing at a beachfront known as Tena Bar, when he discovered three packets of the ransom cash buried in the sandy riverbank. The bills were in poor condition, but still bundled in rubber bands. The money uncovered consisted of two packets of one hundred twenty-dollar bills each and a third packet of ninety, amounting to $5,800 in total, still arranged in the same order as when given to Cooper. Might he, fearing being caught, have decided to bury a small proportion of the loot, as a little nest egg to come back for in case he was apprehended and imprisoned? Whatever the truth, on 8th July 2016, the FBI announced that it was finally suspending active investigation of the Cooper case. It remains the only unsolved case of air piracy in aviation history.

So, what conclusions can we draw with regard to the seemingly inscrutable DB Cooper? Well, the whole operation seems to have been well planned and preprepared. He had good knowledge of both the aircraft and the terrain below, and the fact that he ordered four parachutes was surely to ensure the authorities did not tamper with them, for fear that he would make some innocent party jump with him. Additionally, the hijack took place on Thanksgiving Eve, meaning a four-day weekend lay ahead. Might it have been possible that he was able to complete the hijacking and use the long weekend to get back home in time to go to work on Monday morning as normal? Certainly, the FBI investigation did not reveal anyone who disappeared over that weekend, suggesting the perpetrator could well have simply returned to his day job, albeit as a much wealthier person. For me, it is the fact that no one was hurt and no lives were lost that speaks volumes about the man. Indeed, it seems as though DB Cooper was a thoroughly courteous individual. A latter-day Raffles or Robin Hood, perhaps!

Due to advances in forensic techniques, in 2020, American television series *History's Greatest Mysteries* was able to extract sufficient DNA – taken from a clip-on tie Cooper left behind when he jumped – that identification of the perpetrator ought to be possible if it could be matched with a DNA sample from the hijacker or his descendants. Although the FBI, I am sure, would beg to differ, I, for one, would be a little disappointed if the authorities finally fathom the mystery that is DB Cooper.

SEVEN

THE DISAPPEARANCE OF FREDERICK VALENTICH

Before leaving the subject of aviation in the 1970s entirely, the strange case of Australian pilot Frederick Valentich is another mystery worthy of note. At 6.19pm on 21st October 1978, Frederick took off from Moorabbin Airport, near Melbourne, in a Cessna 182 light aircraft. His plan was to fly west for forty minutes along the Australian coast. Once he reached Cape Otway, he intended to head south over the Bass Strait towards his destination, King Island.

Accounts differ as to the purpose of the flight. According to some reports, he said he was planning to pick up passengers and he did indeed take three spare life jackets with him, which lends credence to this assertion. However, he apparently told others he was going to buy crayfish. As there were no passengers waiting for him at King Island and he had not placed an order for crayfish, both assertions seem to be incorrect. The truth of the matter may, however, be fairly mundane. He was a young man who just liked flying, so he probably made up a couple of different excuses for the evening jaunt. He would possibly have been a little embarrassed to admit the journey had no purpose other than for his own pleasure.

Beginning at 7.06pm, the following is a transcript of a conversation between Frederick Valentich and Steve Robey, an air traffic controller with Melbourne Air Flight Service:

Valentich: Is there any known traffic below five thousand [feet]?
Robey: No known traffic.
V: I am... seems [to] be a large aircraft below five thousand.
R: What type of aircraft is it?
V: I cannot affirm. It is [sic] four bright, it seems to me like landing lights... The aircraft has just passed over me at least a thousand feet above.
R: Roger, and it, it is a large aircraft? Confirm.
V: Er, unknown due to the speed it's traveling. Is there any air force aircraft in the vicinity?
R: No known aircraft in the vicinity.
V: It's approaching right now from due east towards me... [silence for two seconds]. It seems to me that he's playing some sort of game. He's flying over me two, three times, at a time at speeds I could not identify.
R: Roger. What is your actual level?
V: My level is four and a half thousand. Four five zero zero.
R: And confirm you cannot identify the aircraft.

V: Affirmative.
R: Roger. Stand by.
V: It's not an aircraft. It is… [silence for two seconds].
R: Can you describe the, er, aircraft?
V: As it's flying past, it's a long shape. [Silence for three seconds.] [Cannot] identify more than [that it has such speed]. [Silence for three seconds.] [It is] before me right now, Melbourne.
R: And how large would the, er, object be?
V: It seems like it's stationary. What I'm doing right now is orbiting, and the thing is just orbiting on top of me also. It's got a green light and sort of metallic. [Like] it's all shiny [on] the outside. [Silence for five seconds.] It's just vanished… Would you know what kind of aircraft I've got? Is it military aircraft?
R: Confirm the, er, aircraft just vanished.
V: Say again.
R: Is the aircraft still with you?
V: [It's, ah, nor…] [Silence for two seconds.] [Now] approaching from the southwest… The engine is, is rough idling. I've got it set at twenty three twenty four, and the thing is… coughing.
R: Roger. What are your intentions?
V: My intentions are, ah, to go to King Island. Ah, Melbourne, that strange aircraft is hovering on top of me again. [Silence for two seconds.] It is hovering, and it's not an aircraft. [Silence for seventeen seconds, open microphone, with audible, unidentified metallic staccato noise.]
End of transcript.

The conversation with Robey, which ended abruptly

at 7.12pm, was the last time anyone heard from Frederick Valentich. A sea and air search was undertaken that included ocean-going shipping, an RAAF Lockheed P-3 Orion aircraft and eight civilian aircraft. The search encompassed over 1000 square miles. Search efforts continued for four days, but no trace of Frederick or the aircraft was ever found. Five years after Valentich's aircraft went missing, an engine cowl flap was found washed ashore on Flinders Island. However, as a number of Cessna aircraft had been reported as having lost a cowl flap in the general vicinity, it was not possible to identify it as having belonged to the missing aircraft.

Frederick Valentich.

So, what happened to Frederick Valentich? Although he was just twenty years old, he had amassed about 150 total hours' flying time and he held a class-four instrument rating, which authorised him to fly at night. Although he did not have a huge number of flying hours under his belt, he was considered reasonably experienced, given his comparative youth. Various theories have been put forwards to provide a logical

A Cessna 182.

explanation of what happened to Frederick on that fateful evening. One suggestion was that Valentich became disorientated and was flying upside down. If this were the case, the lights he thought he saw would be his own aircraft's lights reflected in the water and he would then, presumably, have crashed into the water.

However, the model of Cessna he was piloting could not have flown inverted for long as it has a gravity feed fuel system, meaning that its engine would have cut out very quickly. Another alternative theory proposed was that Frederick was deceived by the illusion of a tilted horizon for which he attempted to compensate and inadvertently put his aircraft into a downward, so-called 'graveyard spiral'. However, this theory required him to have mistaken the planets Venus, Mars and Mercury, along with the bright star Antares, as the lights from the other aircraft. Extremely unlikely, especially as it was not even dark at the time. There was even a suggestion that he committed suicide. However, interviews with doctors, colleagues and others who knew him, including his father and girlfriend, virtually eliminated this likelihood.

What we are left with reminds me of a phrase coined by Sir Arthur Conan Doyle and attributed to his fictional detective, Sherlock Holmes: 'When you have eliminated the impossible, whatever remains, however improbable, must be the truth'. Did Frederick Valentich really encounter an unidentified flying object that abducted both him and his little plane? It has been over forty years since his disappearance and, to date, it seems about as likely a possibility as the alternative theories.

EIGHT

GOD'S OWN DIVER

If you ever get the chance, Winchester Cathedral in Hampshire, England is well worth a visit. The present cathedral dates from 1079 and replaced the old minster, which had been founded as early as 642. One of the largest cathedrals in Europe, it boasts the largest nave and greatest overall length of any European gothic cathedral. The new cathedral was consecrated in 1093, but unfortunately the building's tower collapsed just fourteen years later. Collapsing towers were a common problem in early English cathedrals and are thought to have been the result of architects failing to take into account the additional weight of the much taller and heavier towers, when laying foundations. Fortunately, the tower was soon replaced and still stands proudly over Winchester today, at a height of 150 feet.

The cathedral was fortunate to have survived the reign of King Henry VIII, who seized control of the Catholic Church in England and declared himself

Winchester Cathedral.

head of the newly founded Church of England in 1534, following a dispute with the papacy. During this period, many religious buildings, particularly monastic ones, were seized by the crown and large numbers were destroyed.

Winchester Cathedral was not so fortunate a century later, however, when – following the outbreak of the English Civil War in 1642 – the huge medieval stained-glass West Window was smashed to pieces by parliamentarian forces. The subsequent victory for parliament and the consequential regicide of King Charles I in 1649 was followed by a period of puritanical rule by Oliver Cromwell, who assumed the grand title of Lord Protector of the Commonwealth of England, Scotland and Ireland until his death in 1658. By 1660, however, the country had grown tired of the austere nature of the government and so the son of the executed king was duly restored to the throne as King Charles II.

Following the restoration of the monarchy, the good people of Winchester gathered up the broken pieces of stained glass and duly reassembled the window. However, no attempt was made to replicate the images that had once shone so spectacularly from the original fenestra. Instead, the pieces were assembled in an arbitrary, haphazard manner, resulting in the stained-glass equivalent of a patchwork quilt! Kind observers might refer to it as a collage, however, notwithstanding the unorthodox reconstruction, there is no doubt that the overall effect is quite striking.

The next two and a half centuries at the cathedral would pass in a relatively orderly fashion. That was until early in the 20th century, when it was observed that floor surfaces were beginning to subside and large cracks began to appear in the walls of the grand old building. TG Jackson, one of the most distinguished architects of his generation, was called in and established that the cathedral had been built on peat – a marshy, organic kind of soil – and that the foundations of the south and east walls were beginning to sink slowly into the ground.

William Walker was born in Newington, Surrey, England in 1869. Little seems to be known about

West Window.

his early life, until he began training as a diver at Portsmouth Dockyard in 1887. He progressed steadily through the roles of diver's attendant and diver's signal man, before passing both a medical and his deep-water test to qualify as a deep-water diver in 1892.

Now, I know what you're thinking: *All very well, but what on earth has this diver bloke got to do with Winchester Cathedral?* Well, quite a lot as it happens! The cathedral was in imminent danger of collapse and urgent remedial work needed to be undertaken. Approximately 235 pits were dug along the southern and eastern walls to a depth of about 6 metres (20 feet) to enable the foundations to be underpinned.

The problem was that the pits immediately filled with water, seeping in from the surrounding peaty soil. The removal of this groundwater would have resulted in the collapse of the building, so an unprecedented method of working would be required if the cathedral was to be saved. Yes, that's right, the work would need to be carried out underwater!

The man chosen for this painstaking, laborious work, was, of course, William Walker. He would need to work at a depth of approximately 20 feet in complete darkness, as the water in the pits contained so much sediment that light could not penetrate more than a few inches. Between 1906 and 1911, working for six hours a day, William single-handedly shored up Winchester Cathedral with more than 25,000 bags of

William Walker – John Crook.

concrete, 115,000 concrete blocks and 900,000 bricks. Once Walker had completed his gargantuan task, the groundwater was finally pumped out and conventional bricklayers moved in and restored the damaged walls.

On completion of the work, a thanksgiving service was held on 15th July 1912, led by the Archbishop of Canterbury. At the service, William was presented with a silver rose bowl by King George V in recognition of his exemplary service. According to contemporary newspaper reports, the king and William were already known to one another, as when the former had been a naval cadet, the latter had been his diving instructor.

When asked about his work on the cathedral, Walker modestly noted: "It was not difficult. It was straightforward work, but had to be carefully done." TG Jackson, however, was more effusive with regard to William's efforts, telling him that he had done what no other man had done – namely that he had single-handedly laid the foundation of an entire cathedral. Walker is said to have replied: "I am proud of the honour."

Bust of William Walker at Winchester Cathedral – Jan Kameníček.

Walker was twice married and fathered several children while working at Winchester Cathedral – at the weekends, presumably! Sadly, William fell victim to the Spanish Flu epidemic and died in 1918, aged just forty-nine. A bust of William Walker, commemorating his great achievement, was erected in Winchester Cathedral and resides there to this day, keeping a watchful eye on those troublesome walls, no doubt!

NINE

THE GHOST WHO SOLVED HIS OWN MURDER?

On 13th February 1936, a passer-by spotted a mangled corpse, lying on rocks in shallow water, underneath the Morandi Bridge in the Italian city of Catanzaro. The body was quickly identified as that of Giuseppe 'Pepe' Veraldi, a local young man. Despite protestations from the man's family that he had been in good spirits and not in the least suicidal, authorities concluded that he had most probably decided to end his life by leaping from the bridge. As his injuries appeared consistent with a fall from a great height, the matter was laid to rest, along with Pepe, and foul play was not suspected. The tragedy initially drew the attention of local newspapers, although, with the exception of those closest to the deceased, the incident soon faded from the collective memory of the community.

Fast forward three years and things started to get weird. In January 1939, Maria Talarico, a local teenager, was wandering over the Morandi Bridge when she claimed she suddenly felt compelled to walk to the very spot from which Veraldi had apparently leapt to his death. Thereupon she became light-headed and passed out. The unconscious young lady was discovered, brought home and put to bed, where she slept for several hours. A doctor called by her concerned parents was mystified, as he could find nothing wrong with the girl to explain her apparent malaise.

When she eventually awoke, all was not as it should have been. She spoke in a low male voice and claimed to be Pepe Veraldi – the dead man. Maria, or Pepe as she now insisted on being called, announced that she, or he, needed to see Pepe's mother as a matter of urgency. He/she also demanded cigarettes, wine and playing cards. These requests would have been most out of character for Maria, who was a teenage girl who didn't drink or smoke, but not, apparently, for Pepe. The family of Maria were understandably alarmed at these strange developments and so, at a loss to know what to do for the best, they decided to contact Catarina Veraldi, Pepe's mum, and ask her to come over. Catarina, assuming this was some kind of sick prank, came anyway to see for herself what all the commotion was about. However, when she arrived, she quickly formed the opinion that Maria had indeed been possessed by the spirit of her dead son. Not only did she recognise his voice, but Maria's handwriting now also resembled that of Pepe.

Maria Talarico.

The purpose of the possession soon became apparent when the spirit of Pepe's mood became dark and he told his mother that he had not committed suicide, but had been murdered by a group of four people he had thought were his friends. He had, he said, been beaten and thrown to his death from the bridge. Having imparted this information to Catarina, the girl then apparently rushed out of the door and ran back to the bridge, and upon reaching the point where the tragedy took place, passed out once more. Those present at Maria's house followed her to the bridge and Pepe's mother beseeched him to leave the poor girl in peace. Subsequently, Maria came to and seemed to be her old self once more, with no recollection of what had just occurred.

With no proof of murder and no idea which so-called friends he might have been referring to, there was little to be done. The police were certainly not going to entertain the notion that a ghost or spirit had returned from the dead to put the finger on his killers. And so that would probably have been that, were it not for a truly bizarre turn of events that took place nine years after the alleged possession of Maria. One day, Catarina received a letter from an old friend of Pepe's called Luigi 'Toto' Marchete. Marchete had emigrated to Argentina shortly after Veraldi's death and in his letter he confessed to murdering Pepe, along with three accomplices, in a fit of jealousy over a woman – just as Pepe, through Maria, had claimed.

Apparently, Marchete had written the letter some time previously and had placed it in an envelope addressed to Catarina Veraldi, with strict instructions that it was to be mailed to her in the event of his death.

As he had subsequently passed away, the letter was duly sent as instructed. His will also left all his assets to Catarina in atonement for her loss at his hands. Now, the police were interested. The case was reopened and the three surviving culprits were quickly apprehended, charged with murder and subsequently convicted.

So, what conclusions can we draw from such an astonishing series of events? If accounts are to be believed, Maria was a young teenager at the time of her involvement and had never heard of Pepe Veraldi or of his supposed suicide three years previously, let alone the exact spot on the bridge from where he had been thrown. The most likely explanation is that the supposed possession was some kind of hoax. Pepe's friends and relatives never accepted the suicide hypothesis and may well have harboured suspicions as to the perpetrators of the crime, leading them to stage a dramatic deception in the hope of reigniting the interest of the wider public and the authorities in the case. On the other hand, it seems remarkable that the hoaxers got it pretty well spot on, correctly identifying the number of assailants involved despite the fact that there were no witnesses.

So, if not a hoax, what are we left with? Did Maria either possess some kind of precognitive ability to foresee the contents of a letter nine years in advance or had she some kind of extrasensory ability to perceive a past event she had not personally witnessed? Or did the ghost or spirit of Pepe Veraldi really take temporary possession of Maria Talarico, in order to make the terrible truth known and to seek justice for his murder? As the killing took place in the mid-1930s, most, if not all, of those involved will have long since passed away themselves, taking any secrets with them to their graves. Ultimately, I guess it will depend on your point of view, whether cynic, sceptic or believer in things paranormal. Whichever way you lean, a remarkable story nonetheless.

TEN

THE EXTENDABLE CLARENCE WILLARD

In 1913, while Clarence Willard was staying in England, he needed to renew his passport in order to be able to travel and, most importantly, in order for him to be able to return to the United States – his country of origin. Consequently, Clarence popped into the US Embassy in London, in order to complete the necessary paperwork. Embassy clerk Edward Hobson was the employee tasked with filling in the documentation. At first, all went well. His questions about date and place of birth, hair and eye colour, and approximate weight were all answered by Clarence in unremarkable fashion. However, when asked for his height, Willard gave the astonishing reply: "Oh, anywhere from 5 feet 9¾ inches to 6 feet 4."

Hobson gave Willard a look of incredulity, obliging Clarence to offer something by way of explanation. "I'm Willard, the man who grows. I will show you what

I mean," he said and, according to a contemporary newspaper report, he 'began slowly to grow, increasing in height until, instead of looking straight into the eyes of Hobson, who is a medium-sized man, he was gazing down at the top of the clerk's head. Hobson called in Frank Page and Harold Fowler, the American Ambassador's son, and private secretary, and for their edification Willard gave a regular side-show in the reception room of the embassy, telescoping up and down apparently with the greatest ease. Page and Fowler inspected the man carefully, feeling his legs in an attempt to find hidden springs or other mechanical apparatus, but they were finally convinced that he was only a freak.'

It seems the remarkable young man possessed the extraordinary ability to be able to elongate himself at will. Clarence Willard was born in 1882 and hailed from Painesville, Ohio. So, what was it about this exceptional individual that gave him his freakish ability? In the September 1927 issue of *Science of Invention*, the magazine set out to explain how Willard grew on command. Editors took him for X-rays and determined that his spinal curvature is 'perhaps greater than that of the average man. By purely muscular exertion he is able to cause the vertebrae to assume a nearly perfect straight line. In this way he can extend the length of his neck. By training, Mr. Willard has been able to increase this movement so markedly that his demonstration is daily surprising thousands'. He actually claimed to have developed the skill in childhood in order to compensate for a left side that was entirely paralysed.

Apparently, Clarence found that he was able

to increase his height by carrying out particular exercises. Although history does not seem to have recorded his exercise regime, the 1978 *Guinness Book of Records* stated that it was through 'constant practice in muscular manipulation of the vertebrae'. However, in 1958, Willard explained to a Society of American Magicians meeting that by carrying out stretching exercises, he could also separate his hip bones and ribs. He found that through a combination of these means, he could add 7½ inches (19cm) to his natural height of 5 feet 9¾ inches (177cm). He was also able to extend the length of his arms by 8–15 inches (20–38cm) and make one leg 4 inches (10cm) longer than the other.

Of course, there would be little point in him being a human precursor to Stretch Armstrong, if he were not to turn this remarkable capability to his advantage. Consequently, from a comparatively early age, Clarence began a career as a freak act vaudeville entertainer. He began performing with the Barnum & Bailey Circus, inviting a volunteer from the audience to join him on stage. He would always pick someone taller than himself. Standing next to each other, Willard would stretch himself until he became the taller of the two. Willard later became associated with Robert Ripley and his *Ripley's Believe It or Not!* newspaper panel series, television show and radio show, which featured odd facts from around the world. Willard was one of a group of freak act performers who appeared at Ripley's odditoriums, and he would also make appearances at other venues across the United States, Canada and Europe. Willard appeared in the 1930 short film *Believe it or Not #3*, introduced by Ripley when challenged (in the film's story) by a journalist to prove

A Double Negative Photograph of Clarence Willard

the quality of his acts. Clarence also performed at the 1936–37 Great Lakes Exposition in Cleveland, Ohio, and even appeared as a guest on *The Ed Sullivan Show*.

Later in life, according to an article in the 3rd December 1956 issue of *Life* magazine, Willard moved to Alameda, California, where he managed real estate and ran a restaurant named the Brass Rail. He continued to perform his elongation routine for customers, presumably without putting them off their dinners. Clarence Willard died on 31st July 1962 at a hospital in Oakland, California, and was buried at the Golden Gate National Cemetery. The size of coffin required was not recorded.

One of the most amusing stories related by Clarence concerned a time he was visiting Spain. According to Willard: "In Madrid in 1912, I was watching a parade. As King Alfonso approached, I stretched a few inches to get a better look. A woman saw me and screamed. The crowd stared and left me standing all alone."

ELEVEN

TITANIC TWICE?

On a cold April night in the North Atlantic, the largest ship ever constructed struck an iceberg on her starboard side and sank, approximately 400 nautical miles off the coast of Newfoundland, Canada. Of the 2,500 passengers and crew on board the stricken vessel, only thirteen survived. The leviathan, which was 800 feet in length and displaced 45,000 tons, was described as 'unsinkable', which was probably the reason why she had been equipped with only twenty-four lifeboats – capable of carrying less than half of her total complement of 3000.

Despite being the largest vessel ever built, due to the use of innovative triple screw propellers, the ship was capable of an astonishing 25 knots at full power, which was exactly the speed she was travelling when she struck the iceberg a glancing blow.

If all this sounds familiar, it is hardly surprising as it is, of course, instantly recognisable as a description of the 20th century's most infamous maritime disaster: the sinking of the *Titanic*. The only trouble is, it isn't! The catastrophic collision between ship and iceberg described above is a work of pure fiction. Be that as it may, the tale borrows so heavily from the actual events of 15th April 1912 that the author could hardly be credited with a fertile imagination! Indeed, one may even go so far as to accuse the writer of profiting from tragedy.

Certainly that would be fair comment, except for one thing: the book in question was published in 1898, a full fourteen years before the *Titanic* plunged to the depths of the North Atlantic Ocean. In fact, when the book was written, the ship that would become the RMS *Titanic* had not even been conceived. So, who was the potentially clairvoyant author, and how accurately did he describe the events of that notorious night, well over a decade before they actually occurred?

The author was one Morgan Robertson, a former seaman and diamond setter, who turned to writing sea tales once his eyesight began to deteriorate as a result of years spent setting precious stones into items of jewellery. Born in 1861, Robertson was never a prolific writer, but nevertheless penned a short novel titled *Futility*, which would come to be regarded as his magnum opus, in which a British passenger liner he called the SS *Titan* sank after striking an iceberg. The hero of the story is a character named John Rowland, who saves the life of the daughter of a former lover, by jumping onto the iceberg with her after the collision. The pair are eventually rescued by a passing ship.

The novel was first published in 1898, but was reissued after the sinking of the *Titanic*, with a new title of *The Wreck of the Titan*. So, could this work really be considered an example of precognition (the knowledge of a future event or situation, especially through extrasensory means)? To this end, let us take a look at the similarities between Robertson's work of fiction and the actual facts relating to the real sinking.

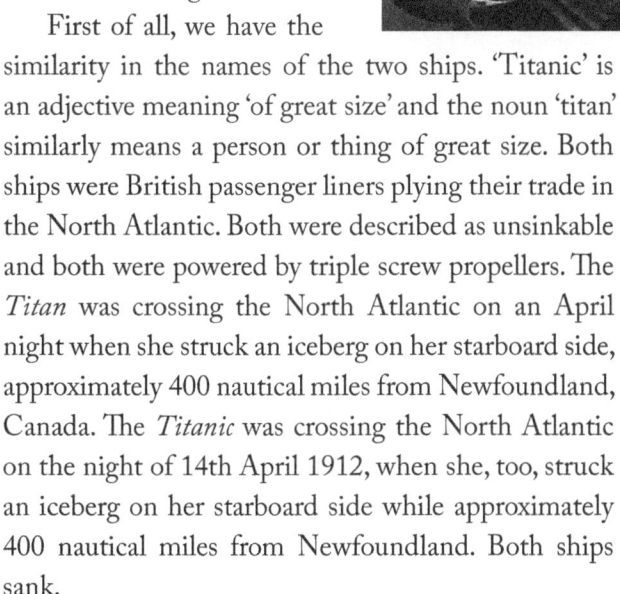

First of all, we have the similarity in the names of the two ships. 'Titanic' is an adjective meaning 'of great size' and the noun 'titan' similarly means a person or thing of great size. Both ships were British passenger liners plying their trade in the North Atlantic. Both were described as unsinkable and both were powered by triple screw propellers. The *Titan* was crossing the North Atlantic on an April night when she struck an iceberg on her starboard side, approximately 400 nautical miles from Newfoundland, Canada. The *Titanic* was crossing the North Atlantic on the night of 14th April 1912, when she, too, struck an iceberg on her starboard side while approximately 400 nautical miles from Newfoundland. Both ships sank.

Morgan Robertson (1861–1915) – taken by George G. Rockwood between 1890 and 1900.

Both vessels were the largest ever constructed and were of very similar size and weight. The *Titanic* was 882 feet long to *Titan*'s 800 feet, and *Titanic* displaced 46,000 tons compared to *Titan*'s 45,000 tons. *Titanic* was travelling at 22.5 knots when the collision occurred, only slightly slower than the 25 knots *Titan* was managing at the time she sideswiped the iceberg. Both ships carried too few lifeboats for the number

A Depiction of the Titanic Disaster – Willy Stöwer.

of passengers and crew aboard, although the outcome of Robertson's tale was more pessimistic, with only thirteen survivors out of a complement of 2,500, compared to 705 survivors of the *Titanic* disaster, out of a total of 2,200 passengers and crew.

After the sinking of the *Titanic*, many were quick to label Morgan Robertson a clairvoyant or soothsayer. However, Robertson himself always denied this, explaining that the similarities were simply due to his knowledge of ships, shipbuilding and maritime trends. Sadly for Morgan Robertson, he was not to enjoy his newfound fame for long. On 24th March 1915, he was found dead of a suspected drug overdose in his room at the Alamac Hotel in Atlantic City, New Jersey. He was just fifty-three years old.

Nevertheless, over a century later, the close correlation between the novel *Futility* and the actual *Titanic* disaster remains astonishing to say the least. Was it all really just a remarkable coincidence or was Morgan Robertson an unwitting recipient of precognition? To this day, the jury remains out!

TWELVE

COLONEL BLOOD AND THE CROWN JEWELS HEIST

If you were ever minded to try and steal the English Crown Jewels, you would have quite a job on your hands. Today, they sit protected by bombproof glass in the Jewel House of the Tower of London, monitored continuously by over a hundred hidden CCTV cameras and overseen by twenty-two Tower Guards. In addition, thirty-eight Yeoman Warders, more commonly known as Beefeaters, who live within the Tower's walls, provide additional security – but it was not always thus. Oh no!

The Crown Jewels went on public display for the first time in 1669, when the Deputy Keeper of the Jewel House, one Talbot Edwards, would, in return for a fee, remove the priceless regalia from their protective repository and show them to visitors. Even by 17th-century standards, this wasn't the most secure method of displaying the nation's valuable assets, you might be thinking – and you'd be right! Indeed, it wasn't long before a certain individual of dubious credentials hatched a cunning plan to relieve the Tower of its treasure.

The superbly named Colonel Thomas Blood had been born in Ireland in 1618 and had fought in the English Civil War for both parliamentarian and royalist sides, although it does not appear that either side actually appointed him to the rank of colonel. It seems that, for reasons best known to himself, he simply adopted the designation of his own accord. However, irrespective of his true status in life, it is for his audacious plot to steal the Crown Jewels that Thomas Blood (colonel or not) sealed his place in British history.

The story begins in the spring of 1671, when, dressed as a parson, Blood paid a visit to the Tower of London, together with a woman whom he claimed to be his wife. They parted with the requisite fee to obtain a viewing of the Crown Jewels, whereupon Blood's supposed wife feigned illness. The sole purpose of this subterfuge was to enable Blood to become acquainted with the aforementioned Talbot Edwards and his family.

The contrived bout of ill health worked a treat and Blood soon returned to the Tower with a gift of gloves for Mrs Edwards,

Colonel(?) Thomas Blood, 1813.

by way of a thank you for her having administered to his wife during her purported malaise. Thomas Blood was thus able to ingratiate himself with the Edwards family and his plan soon moved on to phase three. He made complementary remarks in respect of the Edwards' daughter and announced that his own nephew was wishing to marry, adding that he thought the young lady would make him an excellent wife. According to Blood, his nephew was a man of considerable means and that, were the two to marry, the young lady would be assured of a very comfortable life. Talbot Edwards was suitably impressed and a further visit was duly arranged to enable the matrimonial candidates to meet one another.

That visit took place on 9th May 1671, when Blood, his 'nephew' and a couple of friends arrived for dinner. Despite being seventy-seven years of age and holding a position of considerable responsibility, Talbot Edwards appears to have been somewhat naive. While his wife and daughter were busy preparing the meal, and presumably at Blood's request, he took the four men to the basement where the Crown Jewels were kept.

As soon as they arrived, the gang sprang into action. A cloak was thrown over Edwards, who was then hit with a mallet, stabbed, bound and gagged. The motley crew wasted no time in forcing open the chest containing the jewels and immediately began sharing out the booty. One individual shoved the Orb into his trousers, while another cut the Sceptre in half, as it was too long to fit in the swag bag they had brought with them. In another act of vandalism, Blood battered the crown flat with the mallet, in order that he could depart with the headdress concealed about his person.

However, despite his injuries, the aged Talbot Edwards had been only mildly incapacitated and was thus able to remove the gag, whereupon he raised the alarm by shouting "Treason! Murder! The crown is stolen!" Realising that they had been rumbled, the gang made a run for it. Despite shooting one of the warders, they were nevertheless soon overpowered and Blood and his accomplices were chained and incarcerated in the very castle where they had been dinner guests just a short while earlier.

A Depiction of the Scene of Crime, 1793.

What happened next was remarkable, to say the least. At a time when capital punishment was commonplace, one would have expected Blood to have faced the hangman's noose. However, when Colonel Blood was interrogated, he refused to explain himself, instead stating that he would answer to no one except the king. Surprisingly, King Charles II agreed to interview Blood personally and the prisoner was duly hauled up before the monarch. What persuaded the king towards leniency is not known, but, astonishingly, when he had finished questioning Blood, not only did he pardon him, but he gave him land and an annual income of £500 (over £100,000 in today's terms).

So, why did King Charles II actually reward Blood for what was, on the face of it, an undoubted act of treason? Unfortunately, the truth is unlikely ever to be known, but various suggestions have been put forward to explain the king's extreme benevolence. The least plausible is that he simply took to Thomas Blood and regarded him as nothing more than a loveable rogue. A more conceivable explanation is that Blood was a government spy and was either too valuable to the king to dispense with or was in possession of information pertaining to the king's affairs, which would be damaging if they found their way into the public domain – arrangements for which Blood may have made in advance, in the event of anything untoward happening to him.

Another possibility, albeit ill-conceived, is that the whole thing was basically an inside job! The king was perennially short of cash and, like his father before him, was always looking for ways to raise additional funds. Is it really possible that the king arranged for Blood to steal the Crown Jewels, sell them and add the proceeds to the royal treasury in a sort of early version of a 'Cash for Gold' scheme?

King Charles II with his Crown – Peter Lely.

Whatever the reason, Thomas Blood had only a few years to enjoy his newfound wealth. He died on 24th August 1680, aged sixty-one or sixty-two. Unfortunately for his legacy, it seems as though the king was in the minority in wishing him well, as his epitaph read as follows:

Here lies the man who boldly has run through,

More villainies than England ever knew;
And ne'er to any friend he had was true.
Here let him then by all unpitied lie,
And let's rejoice his time was come to die.

A bit harsh, don't you think?

THIRTEEN

THE ELECTRIFYING ANDREW CROSSE

Andrew Crosse was a wealthy young man, who inherited Fyne Court, a large country house in Broomfield, Somerset, England, at the age of twenty-one in 1805, following the death of his parents, Richard and Susannah. After receiving his inheritance, Crosse, who had been studying law at Brasenose College, Oxford, immediately abandoned his legal studies, in order to devote his time to an altogether different subject.

Andrew Crosse (1784–1855) – unknown

You see, it was at the tender age of twelve that Andrew had been taken to a lecture on the subject of electricity, which had left a lasting impression on the young man. Being of newly independent means, he was thus able to pursue his interest in all things electrical with impunity. Crosse built his own laboratory at Fyne Court where, in about 1807, he began experimenting with electrocrystallisation; a process involving the growth of crystals on electrodes, derived from rocks immersed in various liquids.

Among his other experiments, Crosse constructed an apparatus that incorporated an insulated wire of approximately 1.25 miles in length, suspended from trees and poles, for the purpose of 'examining the electricity of the atmosphere'. He was eventually able to determine the polarity of the atmosphere under various weather conditions. One of his other notable successes was the development of large voltaic piles, the forerunner of the electrical battery. So loud were the reports when he discharged the piles, locals began referring to Crosse as 'the thunder and lightning man'. His work drew the interest of Sir Humphrey Davy, President of the Royal Society, who visited Andrew at Fyne Court in 1827.

Nonetheless, over the years, it would be the subject of electrocrystallisation that he would return to periodically and he would eventually produce a total of twenty-four electrocrystallised minerals. However, it is for what unexpectedly appeared during an electrocrystallisation experiment in 1837 that Crosse is mainly remembered today. He wanted to see if it would be possible to grow crystals by applying only a weak electric current. As days went by without any crystals appearing in the liquid, it appeared that the answer was no.

However, on the 28th day of the experiment, Andrew noticed something that astonished him. Instead of crystals, the liquid now contained numerous tiny insects that resembled mites or fleas. Presuming that his experiment must have become contaminated by microscopic insect eggs, Crosse decided to replicate the experiment using sealed containers in order to eliminate the possibility of contamination. To his amazement, insects once again appeared instead of crystals. He followed this up by repeating the experiment using an assortment of poisonous liquids known to be incapable of supporting life. Astoundingly, on most occasions, insects again emerged from the toxic fluid. Had Andrew Crosse really created life in his laboratory by applying a weak electrical charge to a combination of rock and liquid?

Crosse himself seemed bemused by the results of his experiments. He would later comment: "In fact, I assure you most sacredly that I have never dreamed of any theory sufficient to account for (the insects') appearance. I confess that I was not a little surprised, and am so still, and quite as much as I was when the (insects) first made their appearance… I was looking for (crystal) formations, and (insects) appeared instead…"

Another scientist by the name of WH Weeks decided to try the experiment for himself and even went to the extent of assembling the whole thing inside of a bell jar, to ensure an environment free from external contamination. He, too, noted the appearance of insects, although subsequent attempts by chemist Henry Noad and surgeon Alfred Smee to replicate Crosse's results were not successful.

Crosse identified the insects as belonging to a genus of mites known as 'Acarus' and newspapers who quickly picked up on the story named them 'Acarus Crossii' in his honour. Unfortunately, however, public reaction to Andrew's experiments was not positive.

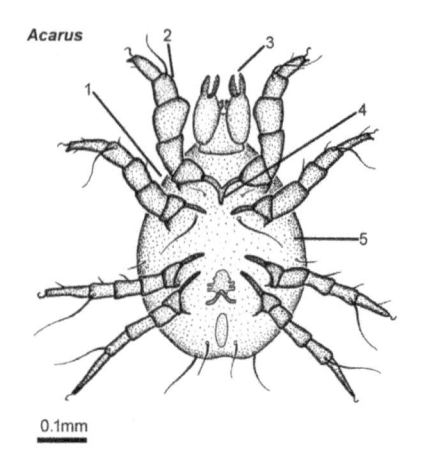

An Example of the Genus Acarus – Acarologiste, own work.

He was accused of fraud, incompetence and, most alarmingly, blasphemy. He was described as being 'a devil, a mere man who dared to make himself equal to the creator God by seemingly creating life out of nothing'. Indeed, such was the furore surrounding Crosse and his work that people began arriving at Fyne Court in order to ridicule him, damage his property and even to perform exorcisms!

Things got so bad for Andrew that he was thereafter rarely seen in public, preferring to spend his time at Fyne Court, avoiding the vitriol that he seemed to attract wherever he went.

On the morning of 26th May 1855, Andrew Crosse suffered a stroke from which he would not recover. He died on 6th July 1855 aged seventy, unusually, in the very same room in which he had been born. He never understood why his work had provoked such a savage reaction from the general public. He was twice married and had ten children, of which three died in childhood.

Subsequent generations of scientists do not appear to have taken Crosse's findings seriously and, in the intervening years, there do not seem to have been any further meaningful attempts to reproduce the results he obtained.

So, what are we to make of all this? The most likely explanation is that, despite his best endeavours, Crosse's instruments had been contaminated by dust mites or something similar. Or is it possible that in the same year that Queen Victoria ascended to the throne, in a laboratory in Somerset, England, a man became a god, just for a while?

FOURTEEN

HELL ON EARTH

In 1981, twelve-year-old Todd Domboski was playing in the backyard of a house in the mining town of Centralia, Pennsylvania, United States, when he suddenly disappeared from view. A sinkhole, 4 feet in diameter and 150 feet deep, had suddenly opened up beneath his feet. Fortunately, the shocked young man was able to cling onto a tree root and he was quickly extricated from the hole by his cousin, fourteen-year-old Eric Wolfgang. Clouds of hot steam soon began billowing from the hole, which, when tested, was found to contain lethal levels of carbon monoxide. It seemed as though Todd had just had a narrow escape from the clutches of hell. So, what on earth was going on beneath the streets of Centralia?

To answer this question, we need to go further back in time – almost twenty years, in fact – to 7th May 1962, when the town council met to discuss the thorny issue of the new Centralia landfill site, which had opened earlier that year, replacing an older refuse dump located close to the town's cemetery. The new site was essentially a pit, approximately 300 feet long by 75 feet wide, and was intended to serve as a single point for all of the town's refuse. It was hoped that this would resolve the problem of fly-tipping, which had long been an issue of concern to the local authority. However, the new dump was filling rapidly and something needed to be done. The most straightforward solution was to simply burn the rubbish in the pit and, although state law prohibited dump fires, the town council nevertheless took the decision to set light to the refuse.

On 27th May 1962, a fire was lit at the landfill site in order to reduce the volume of waste material through combustion. Five members of the local volunteer firefighting service were hired to oversee the process and the dump was allowed to burn throughout the day, with the flames being doused with water at nightfall. Unfortunately, and to the great consternation of the town councillors who had authorised the illegal fire, flames reappeared at the site forty-eight hours after the fire was thought to have been extinguished. A further attempt was made to put out the fire, but on 4th June the rubbish tip flared up again.

This time, a bulldozer was brought in to remove the top layers of refuse so that firefighters could soak the concealed layers of the still-burning waste. However, the removal of several tons of garbage revealed something very disturbing indeed. A hole as wide as 15 feet was discovered in the base of the north wall of the pit, which led to a labyrinth of old mine tunnels under the town. Still the rubbish continued to smoulder and so the council eventually called in Art Joyce, a mine inspector, who brought along gas detection equipment. Tests revealed the presence of carbon monoxide in the still-smoking pit at levels typical of coal mine fires. It transpired that the council's attempt to deal with the town's waste had resulted in the ignition of an underground coal seam.

Unsurprisingly, councillors were keen to absolve themselves of responsibility for the developing catastrophe, so when the Centralia Council sent a letter to the Leigh Valley Coal Company, formally notifying them of the mine fire, they referred to it as being 'of unknown origin during a period of unusually hot weather'. Mine inspectors descended on the town and made daily checks of carbon monoxide levels. When, on 9th August, lethal levels were detected, all Centralia area mines were closed.

The first attempt to deal with the underground fire began in August 1962, through excavation. Unfortunately, this did not help matters, as the digging resulted in the breaching of mine chambers, which allowed oxygen to rush in, further fuelling the fire. This resulted in the fire gaining momentum and moving deeper into the coal seam, faster than the excavators could chase it. By 29th October, the project had run out of money and was halted. Despite the excavation of 58,580 cubic yards of earth, the fire continued to rage on under Centralia.

A second project was proposed, which entailed flushing the mines ahead of the fire with a mixture of water and crushed rock. This, too, failed to halt the fire, as winter had by now set in and unseasonably low temperatures had caused water supply lines to freeze, and the rock grinding machine also froze up. Funding for this project ran out on 15th March 1963. On 11th April, steam was observed emanating from additional fissures in the ground, indicating that the fire was continuing to spread in an easterly direction. A third project involving the digging of trenches to encircle the burning coal seam was also abandoned in 1963.

Despite the closing of the mines and the underground fire, life in Centralia carried on as normal for many years. It seemed as though the townsfolk had largely forgotten about the subterranean conflagration – out of sight, out of mind. However, in 1979, John Coddington, gas station owner and mayor of Centralia, inserted a dipstick into one of his underground tanks to check the fuel level. When he pulled it up, it seemed hot. On lowering a thermometer into the tank, he was shocked to discover the temperature of the fuel to be a worrying 77.8 centigrade. And when in 1981, young Todd Domboski almost lost his life to a steaming

Centralia before and after the demolition of properties.

sinkhole, it became apparent that drastic action would need to be taken.

Even so, progress was slow. In 1984, Congress allocated over $42 million to relocate the residents of Centralia. Most of the population accepted buyout offers and moved away, although a few families opted to stay, despite being warned that the area was no longer a safe environment in which to live. In 1992, all properties within the town were condemned and most were subsequently demolished. In 2002, the US Postal Service revoked Centralia's ZIP code. At the time the fire took hold, the town's population stood at about 1,500. As of 2013, only seven remained, and on 29th October of that year, those remaining residents were given special dispensation, allowing them to live out the remainder of their lives in the properties they had refused to leave.

At the time of writing, the Centralia mine fire has been burning for over fifty-seven years and it is estimated that it could continue to burn at its current rate for at least another 250 years. Surprisingly, no one was ever prosecuted for the illegal dump fire that resulted in the annihilation of an entire town.

FIFTEEN

THE CURSE OF FLIGHT 191

On 5th March 1963, Aeroflot Flight 191, a USSR domestic passenger flight from Vnukovo International Airport, was attempting to land at Ashgabat International Airport in a dust storm. Owing to the weather conditions, the flight ought to have been diverted elsewhere; however, the option to divert was neither suggested by air traffic control nor requested by the pilots. The landing was a disaster. The aircraft skidded on the runway, lost both of its wings and the cockpit was completely destroyed. The fuselage tipped over on its left side and a fire destroyed the entire middle section of the airliner. Of the fifty-four people on board, all eight cockpit crew members died along with four passengers.

The X-15 was an experimental hypersonic rocket-powered aircraft, operated by the United States Air Force between 1959 and 1968. On 15th November 1967, X-15 Flight 191, piloted by Michael J Adams, was ten minutes and thirty-five seconds into its test flight over Randsburg, California, USA, when it got into technical difficulties and broke apart, killing the sole occupant of the airplane.

Prinair (Puerto Rico International Airlines) Flight 191 was flying from Luis Muñoz Marín International Airport in San Juan, Puerto Rico, to Mercedita International Airport in Ponce, Puerto Rico. At the controls were Captain Donald Price, aged twenty-eight, and First Officer Gary Belejeu, who was twenty-seven at the time. At approximately 11.15pm on 24th June 1972, the aircraft attempted to land at Mercedita International Airport. As the flight was late at night, the airport control tower was closed and, as a consequence, the flight crew had sole responsibility for the landing clearance. Just after touching down on the runway, Price and Belejeu were not happy with the situation, so took the decision to go around, meaning they would take off again and circle the airport before landing. However, the pilot over-rotated the aircraft and caused it to stall at a low level and crash. Three passengers and the two flight crew were killed, and the other fifteen passengers were injured. The subsequent air crash investigation cited pilot error as the main cause of the accident, although heavy fog was also listed as a contributing factor.

American Airlines Flight 191 was a scheduled passenger flight from O'Hare International Airport in Chicago, Illinois, USA to Los Angeles International Airport in Los Angeles, California, USA. On 25th May 1979, the McDonnell Douglas DC-10 was taking off from O'Hare's runway 32R, when the left engine detached from the wing. This catastrophic

American Airlines McDonnell Douglas DC-10.

failure caused the aircraft to roll to the left and resulted in it crashing in a field by a trailer park, near the end of the runway. The loss of the engine was the result of damage to the pylon structure holding the engine to the wing, caused by improper maintenance procedures. All 258 passengers and thirteen crew on board were killed, along with two people on the ground. At 273 fatalities, it is, to date, the deadliest aviation accident to have occurred in the United States.

On 2nd August 1985, Delta Air Lines Flight 191 was coming into land at Dallas/Fort Worth International Airport in Texas, USA during a thunderstorm. While approaching the runway, the aircraft encountered a microburst. A microburst is an unusual weather phenomenon, which produces a column of sinking air that is capable of producing damaging winds of over 240 km/h (150mph), often producing damage similar to that of a tornado. The downdraft forced the airplane into the ground and it impacted over 1 mile (1.6km) short of the runway, struck a car near the airport, collided with two water tanks and disintegrated. The crash killed 137 people and injured twenty-six. The National Transportation

Safety Board determined that the crash resulted from the flight crew's decision to fly through a thunderstorm, the lack of procedures or training to avoid or escape microbursts, and the lack of hazard information on wind shear.

On the morning of the 27th August 2006, at around 6.07am, Comair Flight 5191 crashed while attempting to take off from Blue Grass Airport in Fayette County, Kentucky, USA. The aircraft had been assigned the airport's runway 22 for the take-off, but – inexplicably – the pilot used runway 26 instead. Runway 26 was too short for a safe take-off for the Bombardier Canadair Regional Jet 100ER being used for the flight and, consequently, the aircraft overran the end of the runway before it could become airborne. It crashed just past the end of the runway, killing all forty-seven passengers and two of the three crew. The National Transportation Safety Board concluded that the likely cause of the crash was pilot error.

JetBlue Flight 191 was a scheduled domestic commercial passenger flight from New York to Las Vegas, USA. On 27th March 2012, the Airbus A320 diverted to Rick Husband Amarillo International Airport in Amarillo, Texas, after the captain suffered a mental breakdown and began behaving erratically. Captain Clayton Osbon was locked out of the cockpit by First Officer Jason Dowd and was restrained by passengers after he started acting irrationally, ranting about terrorists and 9/11. Fortunately, on this occasion, there were no fatalities.

These incidents have caused the number 191 to be seen by some as unlucky in the aviation industry and, as a consequence, many commercial airlines no longer use it as a flight number. However, some still do. So, you have been warned. If you book yourself on a flight and discover its flight number is 191, you might like to consider an alternative ground-based form of transport instead.

SIXTEEN

THE STRANGE CASE OF THE ACTRESS AND THE SKELETON

Ada Constance Kent was an English actress who enjoyed a degree of success in both stage and screen productions in the early decades of the 20th century. Given her relative fame at the time, it is rather surprising that comparatively little seems to be known about her early life. Ada was born around 1880 and appears to have spent most of her working life in and around London. However, it is not for her thespian accomplishments that she is remembered today.

At some point in her later life, Ada decided to essentially retire from her acting career and retreat from public life. She bought herself a quaint little cottage in the English countryside, in a small village called Fingringhoe, Essex. Rather surprisingly, given her profession and public persona, she never married and turned into something of a reclusive spinster. Ada

THE STRANGE CASE OF THE ACTRESS AND THE SKELETON

Ada Constance Kent.

rarely left the confines of her cottage, with her only regular outing being to frequent the nearby Whalebone pub for a drink and to purchase a packet of Woodbine cigarettes – her preferred choice of smoke.

On 6th March 1939, she popped into the pub as usual for a quick drink and a packet of cigarettes. Although he didn't know it at the time, Alfred J Hasler, landlord of The Whalebone, would be the last person to ever see Ada Constance Kent alive. Unfortunately, due to her reclusive lifestyle, it was a full three months before anyone grew concerned for her welfare. The local police were informed and asked to investigate. They duly dispatched Bernard Constable (yes, he really was Constable Constable) to pay a visit to Ada's cottage, which he did along with Ruben G Winkel – a local gardener.

Quite why the police felt the need to bring a gardener with them has never been adequately explained. They found the place unoccupied, but – other than the missing actress – everything seemed to be in order. On the kitchen table was a tray with a meal waiting to be eaten and next to her chair beside the fireplace was an open copy of *Romeo and Juliet*. Her coat and personal belongings were present and nothing appeared to be missing, save for Ada herself. There was no sign of the property having been broken into, no evidence of a struggle nor any suggestion of foul play.

With nothing to suggest any criminal activity, the property was left untouched, pending the return of the missing occupant. Three years later, in 1942, an old friend of Ada's, George Wynkoll, visited the cottage to look for clues as to her disappearance. He apparently conducted a thorough search of the small home, even checking under furniture for the slightest indication of what had become of his old acquaintance, but without success. He also noted the meal and open book. He commented: "It appears Ada just vanished and never returned."

And so that appeared to be that. A strange and unusual disappearance, for sure, but hardly unique. Unfortunately, people do go missing from time to time and sadly some are never found. However, this particular case was to take a bizarre turn. In March of 1949, a full ten years after Ada was last seen alive, her bank contacted the police, as large sums of money had been deposited into her account – the last being in September 1948. The bank had been trying to contact the account holder without success and so decided to pass the matter onto the local constabulary.

Prompted by the bank's new information, the police decided to have another ferret around Ada's cottage – only this time, they made a shocking discovery. In the bedroom, lying next to the bed, was a fully clothed skeleton. As if to add to the freakishness of the scene, next to the fleshless cadaver was an empty bottle marked 'Poison'. Other than that, however, the rest of the cottage looked just as it had a decade earlier, with one exception. Ada's jewellery and money remained where she had left them, so burglary was ruled out, but oddly the book was gone.

This latest twist made the story front-page news and reporters rapidly descended on the sleepy village. With the local police at something of a loss as to what to make of the latest developments, Scotland Yard took over the investigation. Despite the initial inquest ruling that the bones belonged to the sixty-nine-year-old former actress, the police concluded that the skeleton was not that of Ada Constance Kent as it was too large and was, in all probability, that of a male.

However, other than ruling out the skeleton as being Ada's, England's finest detectives were unable to shed any more light on the mystery. And so, over eighty years after her disappearance, a mystery it remains. What really did happen to Ada? Whose skeleton was found in the cottage and why was it placed there with a bottle marked 'Poison'? Who deposited the money into her bank account and why? And what happened to Ada's copy of *Romeo and Juliet*? Someone, somewhere must have known the answers to some, or possibly all, of these questions. However, given the passage of time, they will by now almost certainly have taken that information with them into the hereafter. So ends the strange case of the actress and the skeleton. One of history's little mysteries.

SEVENTEEN

THE REAL EBENEZER SCROOGE

If you ask someone to come up with a character from a Charles Dickens novel, chances are that it might be Ebenezer Scrooge – the wealthy but miserly protagonist from Dickens' classic tale, *A Christmas Carol*, published in 1843. Indeed, such is the fame of the fictitious cheapskate that the very name 'Scrooge' has been subsumed into the English language to define someone who is mean and miserable by nature. His catchphrase, 'Bah! Humbug!' is also frequently used today as an expression of displeasure at traditional Christmas festivities.

But where did Dickens draw his inspiration for such a colossal tightwad? It seems there are a couple of likely candidates for the accolade of the 'real Ebenezer Scrooge'. May I introduce two of England's greatest skinflints: John Elwes and Jemmy Wood.

John Elwes was born in 1714 and inherited two

fortunes of £100,000 and £250,000 on the respective deaths of his father and uncle – a combined value of approximately £26 million in today's terms. A significant amount of money with which to be able to enjoy life to the full, you might be thinking – and, of course, you'd be right. Elwes, however, was not about to let his newfound prosperity go to his head. Quite the reverse, in fact.

So tight-fisted was the wealthy Elwes that he gained a degree of notoriety due to his miserliness. He would go to bed as darkness fell so as to avoid spending money unnecessarily on candles. He refused to buy new clothes, preferring instead to wear such old and ragged outfits that many who saw him mistook him for a beggar and actually gave him money! While easily able to afford to buy his own coach and horses, Elwes even avoided using public transport and would walk, often in the rain, in order to save on fares.

John Elwes (1714–1789).

His culinary habits were also the stuff of legend. His food was often mouldy and he thought nothing of eating putrefied meat. It was even claimed that, on one occasion, he ate a moorhen that he acquired from a rat that had just pulled it from a river! As you might imagine, Elwes viewed property maintenance as an unnecessary frivolity and, consequently, his large country house gradually deteriorated, until it became virtually uninhabitable. A visiting relative found it necessary to move his bed in the night, in order to avoid rainwater pouring on him through holes in the roof.

In 1772, John Elwes stood for election as a Member of Parliament for Berkshire. Surprisingly, he won, despite having forked out just eighteen pence on election expenses! He retained his seat for twelve years, eventually standing down in 1784, when it became apparent that he would need to mount an expensive re-election campaign. On one famous occasion, he even trumped the great Ebenezer himself, by complaining bitterly about birds stealing his hay for nest-building purposes! Unlike Scrooge, however, his frugality seems to have been restricted to his own circumstance. Following his death in 1789, a contemporary wrote: 'To others, he lent much; to himself, he denied everything... I have it not in my remembrance one unkind thing that ever was done by him.'

Despite having died some twenty-three years before Dickens' birth, such was his notoriety that his reputation for stinginess outlived him by decades. Indeed, there is no doubt that Charles Dickens was well aware of the thrifty Elwes, as he even made reference to him in his last novel, *Our Mutual Friend*.

Jemmy Wood, who was born in 1756, shared many traits with his miserly predecessor, wearing the same ragged clothing for years on end and walking to appointments rather than paying for a carriage, despite being the owner of the Gloucester Old Bank and having a net worth of around £900,000 – or around £72 million in current terms. He was even reported to regularly visit Gloucester Docks in order to fill his pockets with small pieces of coal that fell from the boats as they were being unloaded!

Most famously, he once hitched a ride back to Gloucester from Tewkesbury in the back of a hearse, by occupying the space normally reserved for passengers of a more deceased nature. Unlike Elwes, however, Wood's tightfistedness extended into his business affairs and, as a consequence, he was much disliked in the community. When he eventually needed the services of an undertaker for real in 1836, it was reported that his coffin was stoned.

Tales of the Gloucester Miser, as Wood was known, were familiar to Dickens, who also mentions him in *Our Mutual Friend*. In addition, a character by the name of Dismal Jemmy appears in another of Dickens' novels, *The Pickwick Papers*. Even after his death, Jemmy Wood's fiscal fastidiousness persisted. So hotly contested was his will that a protracted court case ensued, resulting in much of his estate being swallowed up in legal fees. It has been suggested that the court case of Jarndyce v Jarndyce in another of Dickens' novels, *Bleak House*, may have been based on the real-life wranglings of Wood's disputed will.

Jemmy Wood (1756–1836).

It is tempting to think that Charles Dickens' fictional character, Ebenezer Scrooge, was something of an exaggerated version of the individuals from whom he drew his inspiration. However, given that it is likely that both Elwes and Wood served as the basis for the miserly Scrooge, when one takes into account the incredible tightfistedness of both men, he probably had to tone it down a bit!

EIGHTEEN

TAMAM SHUD – THE SOMERTON MAN MYSTERY

The weather on 30th November 1948 was pleasant, so a couple decided to take an evening stroll along Somerton Beach near Adelaide, Australia. At about 7pm, they noticed a man lying on the sand with his head propped against the sea wall. He extended his right arm, possibly as a form of greeting, before dropping it limply by his side. As he showed no reaction to the numerous mosquitoes buzzing him, the logical conclusion was that he was simply drunk and had gone to the beach in order to sleep it off.

When the husband of the couple was walking his dog along the beach the following morning at about 6.30am, he was perturbed to find the man still there, lying in the same position. Having established that the man was, in fact, dead, he notified the police, who were quickly in attendance.

An initial search of the man's clothing revealed a

few interesting personal effects. Two tickets, one train and one bus, which did not appear to have been used, were in his pockets, as was a packet of Juicy Fruit chewing gum, an American-type aluminium comb and a box of Bryant & May matches. But perhaps the most perplexing of these finds was an Army Club cigarette packet that contained seven cigarettes of a different, more expensive, brand. To put cheaper cigarettes into a more expensive packet might seem logical, so as to give the impression of smoking better-quality cigarettes, but to do the reverse seems a little odd, unless for some reason he was trying to appear less refined. An unlit cigarette was also found on the lapel of his jacket.

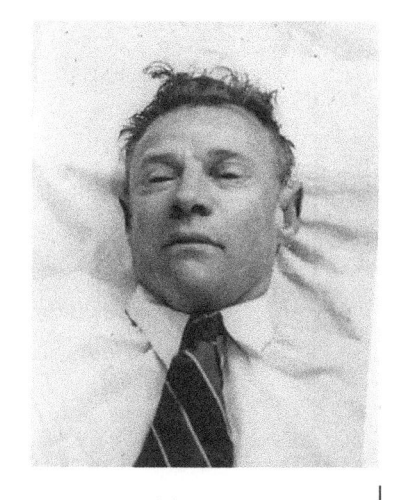

Somerton Man.

The subsequent autopsy failed to reveal a cause of death, as no traces of foreign substances could be detected in the body, although several internal organs were congested and his spleen was approximately three times the normal size. Dr Dwyer, the pathologist who conducted the autopsy, was convinced that the death was not natural and concluded that he believed poisoning to be the most likely cause, with barbiturates or sleeping pills as the most probable candidates. Other than the fact that he was dead, however, the unidentified man seemed to be in excellent physical condition. Aged in his early to mid-forties, he was 5 feet 11 inches tall and had begun to grey slightly around the temples. He had broad shoulders, a narrow waist, pronounced calf muscles and toes that met in a wedge shape, suggesting the physique of a dancer or gymnast, although the tapering toe shape pointed to ballet as the most likely activity.

His clothing was also of interest since, although dressed reasonably smartly – shirt, tie, pullover and a double-breasted jacket – all the labels on his clothes had been removed. He was not carrying a wallet or any means of identification, leading the police to suspect that he had probably committed suicide and did not want to be identified. An examination of his teeth did not match the dental records of any known missing person.

Most enigmatic of all, however, was a tiny piece of rolled-up paper found in the fob pocket of the man's trousers. A fob pocket is basically a small pocket within a pocket, which was popular in the days before wristwatches were commonplace, and was used to hold a pocket watch. However, this fob pocket contained only the small rolled-up scrap of paper, which had to be removed with tweezers. When unrolled, the words 'Tamam Shud' could be seen clearly printed on it. No one at the police department had a clue as to what these words meant and so they eventually turned to the public for help.

A local academic came to their aid. He advised them to obtain a copy of a book called *Rubáiyát of Omar Khayyám*. He went on to explain that the book was a translation of quatrains by the 12th-century Persian poet, Omar Khayyám, and that the last line of the book, which had been left untranslated, was 'Tamam Shud'. Although, as the last line of a book, we would probably translate it as 'The End', a more accurate translation would be: 'It is Finished'. A clear, if concise, suicide note, perhaps?

It appeared that the scrap of paper had, indeed, come from a copy of the book and so another public appeal was made by police, this time to try and find the very copy from which it had been torn. The appeal eventually bore fruit when a man to whom police gave the pseudonym 'Ronald Francis', in order to protect his true identity, produced a copy in which the words 'Tamam Shud' had been torn away. Careful examination revealed a match to the piece of paper found in the man's pocket.

According to police, 'Mr Francis' had found the copy in the rear footwell of his car, which had been parked, unlocked, close to Somerton Beach, around the same time as the discovery of the man's body. He thought it strange, but did not link it to the body on the beach, until the police made their appeal. To add further mystification to the case, in the back of the book were five lines of text handwritten in code. Unfortunately, due to the brevity of the message, there were insufficient repetitions of letters to enable the message to be deciphered. However, a telephone number was also found in the back of the book, which turned out to belong to a nurse by the name of Jessica Ellen Thomson, who lived only about 400 metres north of where the man's body was found.

Thomson was interviewed by police and shown a plaster cast of the dead man's head. She maintained that she did not know the deceased and had no idea why her phone number was in the book. However, those present noted that when shown the plaster bust, she looked shocked and quickly looked away. Jessica died in 2007 at approximately eight-five years of age. If she really did know the identity of the Somerton Man, she took that secret with her to the grave.

However, she left behind a tantalising clue in the form of her eldest son, Robin, who was eighteen months old at the time of the discovery of the body on the beach. The dead man had two unusual anatomical features: a rare genetic dental disorder called hypodontia, found in only about one to two per cent of the general population, and his cymba (upper ear hollow) was larger than his cavum (lower ear hollow), an abnormality present in only about two per cent of individuals. Jessica Thomson's son also had hypodontia, as well as the rare ear configuration. The chances of this being a mere coincidence is estimated as being between one in ten million and one in twenty million. Robin Thomson died in 2009.

The unidentified body of The Somerton Man was laid to rest in Adelaide's West Terrace Cemetery on 14th June 1949. To date, requests for an exhumation to enable DNA testing have been declined. As one might imagine with a case like this, theories and potential identifications abound, ranging from the more fanciful notions that he was a spy or someone wanted for war crimes to the more mundane, such as a missing sailor or railway worker. By 1953, the police had received over 250 suggestions as to the possible identity of the deceased, but no positive identification was ever made.

While his identity may never be known, the most likely scenario would seem to be that he had been in a relationship with Jessica Thomson, which, despite having ended, resulted in the birth of Robin. Jessica had, in the meantime, begun a new relationship with

Prosper Thomson, whom she soon married. Given that Jessica lived close to the beach where the body was found, it seems likely that he visited her and discovered, to his utmost disappointment, that he would not be a part of the lives of his former lover and their son. Dejected, he took his own life. Although we shouldn't forget that Jessica was a nurse. Might his arrival at her new marital home have been an inconvenience to her, necessitating his swift removal from this mortal coil?

Somerton Man Headstone.

The case remains open. But for now:
Tamam Shud.

ADDENDUM

On 26th July 2022, Adelaide University Professor Derek Abbott, in association with genealogist Colleen M Fitzpatrick, claimed to have identified the man as Carl 'Charles' Webb, an electrical engineer and instrument maker, born in 1905. The identification was based on genetic genealogy from DNA of the man, extracted from strands of hair, taken from a plaster death mask made by South Australian Police at the time of the original investigation. Matches were found for descendants of two first cousins of the deceased. South Australia Police and Forensic Science South Australia have not verified the result, but South Australia Police said they were 'cautiously optimistic'. No death record for Webb exists, with his last known records dating to April 1947, when he left his wife.

Webb was also fond of poetry, possibly explaining the link with the *Rubáiyát of Omar Khayyám*. Assuming this identification to be correct, Somerton Man was not the father of Robin Thomson.

NINETEEN

A DEGREE OF ERROR

At 5.15am on 17th July 1938, Irish American pilot, Douglas Corrigan, taxied his dilapidated Curtiss Robin OX-5 monoplane onto the runway of Floyd Bennett Field, an airfield in Brooklyn, New York City, in preparation for a flight to Long Beach, California. At a little over 2,800 miles, the journey westward across the United States would take, Corrigan calculated, about twenty-seven hours. However, he took off in an easterly direction at the request of Kenneth P Behr, manager of the airfield, so as to avoid having to fly over the administration building at the westerly end of the runway.

On 18th July, after a journey of twenty-eight hours and thirteen minutes, the tiny aircraft landed. To his apparent consternation, however, Corrigan soon realised that he was not in Long Beach, California, but almost 6000 miles away at Baldonnel Aerodrome, County Dublin, Ireland. Douglas Corrigan had just crossed the Atlantic Ocean in a rickety old crate of an aircraft! So, what went wrong? Did he just forget that he had taken off in an easterly direction and simply failed to turn around?

For those inclined to believe Corrigan, that is exactly what he maintained happened. However, as you might imagine, all was not quite as it seemed. In 1935, Corrigan had made an application to the Bureau of Air Commerce for permission to make a non-stop transatlantic flight from New York to Ireland, but his application was rejected as his aircraft was deemed to be unsatisfactory for such a flight, although he was able to obtain a lower standard of certification permitting him to make cross-country journeys only.

Douglas Corrigan Standing next to His Aircraft.

Despite his best endeavours, which included the installation of a more powerful 165-horsepower engine in place of the original 90-horsepower motor, additional fuel tanks and other significant modifications, each of his subsequent reapplications for full certification of his aircraft were refused, as the ageing plane was deemed to be unsafe. Indeed, it would appear that the Bureau of Air Commerce were not wrong, as on the inbound flight to Floyd Bennett Field, Corrigan's aircraft developed a fuel leak. Astonishingly, he took the decision to press on with his plans, as he considered that the leak was not too bad, and he was also of the opinion that repairing it would take too long. The very real possibilities of his plane exploding mid-air or running out of fuel during the flight did not seem to bother the single-minded Douglas Corrigan!

About ten hours into his flight, Corrigan felt his feet were getting cold and realised that the leak was getting worse and that, consequently, gasoline was starting to pool in the floor of the cockpit. His solution was to use a screwdriver to make a hole in the floor on the opposite side of the plane from the scorching hot exhaust pipe, so as to let the fuel drain away in comparative safety. He also elected to increase his airspeed by around twenty per cent in order to decrease the time he would need to spend in the air. This course of action has led many to suspect that he knew he was flying over the ocean, as a more prudent approach to the situation – if flying over the United States – would have been to seek out a local airfield to land at and effect a repair.

Obvious comparisons were drawn with Charles Lindbergh, the aviation pioneer who had made the first transatlantic flight eleven years earlier. There were, however, a number of significant differences between the two achievements. Contemporary journalist HR Knickerbocker (yes, that really was his name!) wrote the following in 1941: 'You may say that Corrigan's flight could not be compared to Lindbergh's in its sensational appeal as the first solo flight across the ocean. Yes, but in another way the obscure little Irishman's flight was the more audacious of the two. Lindbergh had a plane specially constructed, the finest money could buy. He had lavish financial backing, friends to help him at every turn. Corrigan had nothing but his own ambition, courage, and ability. His plane, a nine-year-old Curtiss Robin, was the most wretched-looking jalopy. As I looked over it at the Dublin airdrome I really marvelled that anyone should have been rash enough even to go in the air with it, much less try to fly the Atlantic. The nose of the engine hood was a mass of patches soldered by Corrigan himself into a crazy-quilt design. The door behind which Corrigan crouched for twenty-eight hours was fastened together with a piece of baling wire. The reserve gasoline tanks, put together by Corrigan, left him so little room that he had to sit hunched forward with his knees cramped, and not enough window space to see the ground when landing.'

Despite breaking numerous flight regulations, his punishment was extremely lenient; his pilot's certificate was suspended for just fourteen days! Upon his return to the United States by steamship, he was given a ticker-tape parade on Broadway, which attracted more people than had turned out to honour Lindbergh. He was also honoured with an additional ticker-tape parade in Chicago.

Such was his popularity that, in addition to his autobiography, he also starred as himself in a film biography entitled *The Flying Irishman* in 1939. He also endorsed a number of 'wrong-way' products, such as a watch that ran backwards!

Douglas 'Wrong-Way' Corrigan, as he was thereafter known, died on 9th December 1995 at the age of eighty-eight. He was buried at Fairhaven Memorial Park in Santa Ana. Up until his death he always maintained that he had made his transatlantic flight by accident. Yeah, right – if you say so, Doug!

TWENTY

ABANDONED CYPRUS

The beautiful Mediterranean island of Cyprus has a long and chequered history. Of great strategic importance, located as it is just a stone's throw from the Middle East, it has been fought over for centuries and has, at various times, been under the occupation of Greece, Persia, Rome, England, Venice, the Ottoman Empire (Turkey) and the British Empire – to name but a few. However, the purpose of this story is not a deep dive into the turbulent history of the sun-kissed island. Suffice it to say that by the 1970s, Cyprus was an independent nation with a population made up of Greek Cypriots, who formed the majority, and a smaller number of Turkish Cypriots.

The two communities rubbed along in relative harmony until 15th July 1974, when a Greek-led coup d'état ousted the incumbent president, Archbishop Makarios III, in order to unite the island with Greece. In response, on 20th July 1974, Turkey invaded

Northern Cyprus on the pretext of defending the rights of the Turkish Cypriot community, initially landing 6000 troops, as well as tanks and other armoured vehicles. The Turkish Air Force bombed Greek positions and also dropped hundreds of paratroopers in the area between the capital, Nicosia, and the resort of Kyrenia to the north. By the time a ceasefire had been agreed, Turkey had landed 30,000 troops on the island. However, the Greek regime was short-lived and constitutional order was soon restored, with Glafkos Clerides being installed as the new president of the still-independent island.

With the justification for the invasion removed, the United Nations and the international community called for peace negotiations. However, Turkey instead staged a second invasion on 14th August 1974. By the time international pressure was brought to bear, Turkey had occupied almost thirty-seven per cent of the island, 200,000 Greek Cypriots had been forcibly evicted from their homes in the north and 50,000 Turkish Cypriots were displaced from their homes in the south of Cyprus. Most tragically of all, however, was that 1,534 Greek Cypriots and 502 Turkish Cypriots were missing as a result of the fighting. Many of their bodies have never been found. Despite international condemnation, Turkey did not withdraw and instead created the Turkish Republic of Northern Cyprus. The republic is not recognised by the international community and is, even now, considered to be an illegal occupation.

To this day, Cyprus and its capital city of Nicosia remain divided. Indeed, since the fall of the Berlin Wall in 1991, Nicosia is the world's only divided capital city and passports must be shown in order to move between the two sides. There are also a couple of other anomalies that resulted from the Turkish occupation of Northern Cyprus that still exist today. Prior to 1974, Famagusta was not only the number-one tourist destination in Cyprus, but one of the most popular in the world. The rich and famous frequented its beaches and hotels. Regular visitors included celebrities such as Raquel Welch, Brigitte Bardot, Elizabeth Taylor and Richard Burton. The main tourist area of the city was called Varosha and boasted many modern high-rise hotels, such as The King George Hotel, The Grecian Hotel and The Florida Hotel, which adorned John F Kennedy Avenue – an esplanade that ran parallel to the splendid Glossa Beach, with views out to Protaras and Fig Tree Bay.

Following the Turkish invasion in 1974, Famagusta found itself in the occupied sector and, fearing a massacre, the entire population of 39,000 fled Varosha, intending to return when hostilities ended. However, when the invading army took control of Famagusta, they fenced off Varosha, refusing to let anyone enter. Despite a UN Resolution requiring it to be handed over to the administration of the United Nations, Turkey refused to comply, instead using it as a bargaining tool in negotiations towards the international recognition of the Turkish Republic of Northern Cyprus. To this day, Varosha remains a ghost town. Without human occupation, the city has begun to be reclaimed by nature and, without maintenance, the once opulent buildings continue to crumble and decay. Boat and coach trips bring tourists to view the deserted resort from vantage points, but entry remains strictly prohibited.

Varosha As It Is Today.

Prior to the invasion, Nicosia International Airport was the only international airport on the island and included a modern, busy terminal building, serving holidaymakers and business travellers alike. On 20th July 1974, the airport was heavily bombed by the Turkish Air Force, necessitating its immediate and permanent closure. Following the ceasefire in August 1974, the airport became part of the United Nations-controlled Buffer Zone, separating the Greek and Turkish communities, which remains in place today. Consequently, Nicosia International Airport is now the aviation equivalent of a ghost town. The derelict terminal building that once thronged with passengers is now frequented only by pigeons and a stranded Cyprus Airways Hawker Siddeley Trident passenger jet sits forlornly on the tarmac, still patiently awaiting its next complement of passengers.

A new international airport was hastily constructed in Larnaca and opened for business in 1975. A second

Abandoned Passenger Terminal.

Still Awaiting Departure.

international airport followed in Paphos in 1983. On the occupied side of the island, the Turkish Cypriot community opened Ercan International Airport in 2004. However, as this is not recognised by Cyprus or the international community as a legal entry or exit point, only flights to and from Turkey use this facility.

Today, Cyprus remains a popular destination for holidaymakers from Europe and beyond, with major tourist resorts on the Greek side of the island at Paphos, Limassol and Larnaca, plus many charming smaller villages, beaches and bays for visitors to enjoy.

There is also much for lovers of history to explore. The Turkish side of the island remains less developed, although Kyrenia is a beautiful port well worth visiting and Famagusta is a vibrant city, except, of course, for Varosha, where only the ghosts of those long-departed jetsetters wander today.

TWENTY-ONE

HOORAY HENRY

Henry Cyril Paget seemingly had it all. As the eldest son of the 4th Marquess of Anglesey, Henry was heir to his father's title and vast estates, which provided an income of around £12 million per year in current terms. Born on 16th June 1875, a life of privilege was assured for the young aristocrat.

His great-grandfather was Field Marshall Henry William Paget, hero of the Battle of Waterloo. Famously, on losing one of his legs to a cannonball, he is said to have simply exclaimed, "By God, sir, I've lost my leg!" to which his commanding officer, the Duke of Wellington, responded in similar vein with "By God, sir, so you have!" Upon completing his education, young Henry followed in the footsteps of his illustrious predecessor and was commissioned as a Lieutenant in the 2nd Volunteer Battalion of the Royal Welch Fusiliers. Unlike his heroic ancestor, however, military life did not sit well with the youthful nobleman. Indeed, it was to be to an entirely different lifestyle that he found himself drawn.

Married on 20th January 1898 to his cousin, Lilian Florence Maud Chetwynd (1876–1962), Henry soon found himself installed as the 5th Marquess of Anglesey, following the death of his father on 13th October of the same year. Espoused, titled and wealthy, his future could not have seemed rosier. However, all was not quite as it seemed.

The marriage, it transpired, was never consummated and, as a consequence, was annulled after three years. Henry, meanwhile, had begun to enjoy a lavish and eccentric lifestyle. He began to spend his newly acquired fortune on jewellery and furs, as well as hosting lavish parties and staging elaborate theatrical performances. He even converted the chapel on the family estate into an 150-seat theatre, which he named the Gaiety Theatre. Dressed in extravagant and expensive costumes, the marquess always took the lead role, irrespective of his suitability for the part. Productions included, among others: *Aladdin*, Oscar Wilde's *An Ideal Husband*, Shakespeare's *Henry V*, as well as variety performances of sketches and songs and dance routines. Quite an eclectic mix!

He poached actors from London theatres by offering them inflated salaries and eventually took his theatre company on a three-year tour of Britain and mainland Europe. Perhaps most astonishing of all, however, was his 'Butterfly Dance', which he performed during intermissions. Described as 'sinuous', 'sexy' and 'snake-like', he would wave a robe of transparent white silk around like butterfly wings as he danced.

This flamboyant lifestyle, together with the

breakdown of his marriage, led many to speculate that the marquess was homosexual. A contemporary journalist wrote: 'Bearing the form of a man, he yet had all the tastes, something even of the appearance, of not only a woman, but, if the phrase be permissible, a very effeminate woman.' There is, however, no evidence of Henry having any sexual relationships with either men or women, leading historian Viv Gardner to conclude that he was 'a classic narcissist: the only person he could love... was himself'. The lack of evidence may, however, be due to the fact that, after his death, his family destroyed all his papers and personal effects in an attempt to expunge the 5th Marquess from history. Thus, the true nature of his sexuality is not positively known.

Henry Cyril Paget, 5th Marquess of Anglesey.

On the other hand, his extravagant way of life was all too well documented. In the six years since inheriting his title, his outgoings massively exceeded his considerable income – to such an extent that, in June 1904, he was obliged to file for bankruptcy, owing creditors a sum that in today's terms would equate to around £250 million. The estate was remortgaged and an auction arranged to sell off belongings in an effort to repay some of his creditors. Among the items up for auction were jewellery, cars, boats, animals and the world's largest collection of walking sticks. Much of his clothing was also put up for sale and included hundreds of silk dressing gowns and hundreds of pairs of shoes. In total, there were an astonishing 17,000 lots and the auction took forty days to complete. Fortunately for those to whom he was indebted, most got their money back.

Benevolently, his creditors opted not to leave him destitute and awarded him the sum of £3000 per annum – around £150,000 in today's terms – for the remainder of his life. Sadly, however, that was not to be long. Following his bankruptcy, he moved to France, where he contracted tuberculosis. Henry Cyril Paget, 5th Marquess of Anglesey, passed away on 14th March 1905 in the appropriately luxurious surroundings of the Hotel Royale in Monte Carlo at the age of just twenty-nine years. Touchingly, Lilian, his ex-wife, was with him when he died.

Lilian went on to marry a banker in 1909, with whom she subsequently had three children. The title and estate were inherited by his cousin, Charles Paget, who had strongly disapproved of his predecessor's lavish lifestyle and was no doubt miffed that his inheritance had been frittered away. Henry's Gaiety Theatre was reconverted back to a chapel.

TWENTY-TWO

THE MYSTERIOUS DEATH OF ALFRED LOEWENSTEIN

Alfred Leonard Loewenstein was born in Brussels, Belgium on 11th March 1877. His father, Bernard, was a banker and it was no surprise when his son followed in his footsteps. Alfred, however, was a shrewd investor. Many went further, claiming he was unscrupulous or even downright crooked. Regardless of the legitimacy of his business dealings, by the 1920s, Alfred Loewenstein was one of Europe's most powerful financiers and thus was among the richest men in the world at the time.

His business interests ranged from a company providing hydroelectric power facilities to developing countries, to a purported drug deal made with American racketeer, Arnold Rothstein. Apparently, the pair planned to vastly increase the supply of heroin to the United States and in so doing create an international

Alfred Loewenstein.

drug ring throughout Europe and the US. In 1926, he founded a company called International Holdings and Investments Ltd., which raised vast amounts of money from wealthy individuals keen to invest in the business of such a successful man. However, by 1928, they had seen no return on their investments and were rapidly losing patience with the slightly dodgy financier. Alfred Loewenstein may have been wealthy and powerful, but he had his enemies.

It was against this background that on the early evening of 4th July 1928, Alfred climbed aboard his private aircraft at Croydon Airport, England for a comparatively short flight across the English Channel and Northern France to Brussels, where he lived with his wife, Madeleine. Accompanying him on the flight were pilot Donald Drew, mechanic Robert Little, valet Fred Baxter, secretary Arthur Hodgson and stenographers Eileen Clarke and Paula Bidalon. The weather was fine and Drew was expecting a smooth, uneventful flight. Smooth it may have been, but uneventful it certainly wasn't.

At a little after 6pm, the aircraft, a Fokker FVII, was prepared for take-off. A short while later they were airborne and heading out over the Channel. The aircraft was cruising at about 4000 feet when Loewenstein, who had been working quietly, got out of his seat and went to use the lavatory at the rear of the cabin. The configuration of the aircraft was such that the door to the lavatory and the exit door were situated opposite one another, and separated from the main seating area by a third door that opened to a short passageway. Apparently, after about ten minutes had passed, and aware that his employer had not returned to his seat, Fred Baxter went to check on him, fearing that he might have been taken ill. Accounts differ slightly as to what happened next. In one account, Baxter found the toilet cubicle empty and the exit door of the aircraft open and flapping in the slipstream. In another version, Baxter forced open the toilet door only to find it empty, with no suggestion that he found the exit door open. Either way, Alfred Loewenstein was no longer on board the aircraft.

As the Fokker FVII was a light aircraft, an airport runway was not an essential requirement for take-off and landing, and Drew consequently decided to make an emergency landing on – what he determined to be – a deserted beach near Dunkirk. What he hadn't noticed was that, at the time, the beach was also being used by an army unit for training purposes. On seeing the aircraft land, they realised that it must have got into difficulty and rushed to offer assistance, although it took them approximately six minutes to reach the plane and what remained of its passengers and crew. Oddly, the senior officer, a Lieutenant Marquailles, found Donald Drew to be evasive and it took almost thirty minutes of questioning before he admitted that Loewenstein had disappeared from the aircraft while they were flying over the English Channel. The plane eventually took off from the beach, but instead of continuing on to Brussels, it diverted to a local airfield called St. Inglevert, before returning to Croydon.

On 19th July, a body was discovered by fishermen

in the sea near Boulogne. They hauled it aboard their trawler and took it to Calais, where it was identified as that of Alfred Loewenstein by means of his wristwatch. An autopsy was undertaken, which revealed several broken bones as well as a fracture to the skull, although it was concluded that he had been alive when he entered the water.

To date, the question of what actually happened to Alfred Loewenstein remains unanswered, but there are a number of theories, within which the truth almost certainly lies. Clearly his demise was the result of either an accident, suicide or murder; but which?

The most straightforward hypothesis is that he simply opened the wrong door and fell to his death by accident. Many acquaintances of Loewenstein had noted an increasing absent-mindedness in the financier in the months leading up to his death. However, it seems unlikely that he would have obliviously opened a door that was clearly marked as an exit, especially as it would have taken considerable force to do so in flight. Instead, might he have deliberately opened the door and jumped in order to commit suicide? He was certainly under pressure from investors and some have even speculated that as his corrupt practices were about to be exposed, he probably chose death over disgrace and ruin. The weakness of this theory, however, is that no direct evidence linking him to corruption was ever produced.

So, to murder. Loewenstein clearly had enemies, although it did not appear that any association existed between those on board the aircraft and those with whom he had crossed swords in the past. Nevertheless, the inconsistencies in Baxter's account of events and Drew's evasiveness when questioned led many to suspect foul play. It was known that the tycoon's relationship with his wife was not good and it was alleged that she was desperate to get her hands on his vast fortune before things frosted over irrevocably. Might she have plotted with his employees to have him overpowered and thrown out of the aircraft? This theory would certainly account for the skull fracture, although it is also possible that this occurred when he hit the water at considerable speed.

At a distance of almost a century, your guess is as good as mine. However, there is one last interesting twist to the tale, should you be inclined to believe in these things. Mrs EM Taylor, a respected medium at the time, claimed to have been contacted by the spirit of Alfred Loewenstein, whom she alleged made the following statement: "No idea of suicide entered my head till I went to inspect the plane before take-off. Later, I suddenly felt an irresistible impulse to open the door and end my existence. I fought it but each time it grew stronger. A fierce longing took possession of me, which I could not deny. What I went through you will never understand. I longed for death more passionately than a condemned man longs for life. Why, I could not explain. Shall I ever forget that awful plunge into space? Yes, I realised for a moment my mistake, but too late…"

TWENTY-THREE

KORLA PANDIT – THE INDIAN MUSIC MAESTRO?

Unless you hail from the United States and are of a certain age, the name 'Korla Pandit' may not be familiar to you. It certainly wasn't to me. However, despite the fact that I live on the wrong side of the Atlantic Ocean to have been conversant with the career of the talented musician, his story is a fascinating one nonetheless.

Born in New Delhi, India in 1921, Korla Pandit was the son of a French opera singer and an Indian government official. He was raised in an upper-class household and came to England as a child in order to study music. At the age of twelve, he emigrated to the United States, where he went on to study at the University of Chicago. His talent as a keyboard player was soon recognised and, coupled with his exotic Indian background, of which little was known to Americans at the time, he was soon in much demand. By the late 1940s, he was appearing regularly on radio shows, *Chandu the Magician* and *Hollywood Holiday*, and by 1949 he even had his own television programme, *Korla Pandit's Adventures in Music*. As his career developed, his shows became known for the blending of his music and his spiritual ideology – of which he frequently spoke – to the enchantment of his many admirers.

Korla Pandit.

Fame and fortune had come his way and his acquaintances included the actor Errol Flynn, comedian Bob Hope and Paramahansa Yogananda, the Indian spiritual leader of the Self Realization Fellowship. On the nightclub circuit, he often performed with another up-and-coming pianist who went by the name of 'Liberace'. Indeed, it has been suggested that in some ways, Pandit made Liberace into the consummate performer. Little eccentricities, such as occasionally gazing up from the piano to engage the audience, were nuances Liberace took from Pandit's performance and worked into his own. However, by the 1970s, his television work had begun to dry up, so he supplemented his income with personal appearances and concerts. Fortunately, his career was revived in the 1990s, when a new generation of followers were attracted to his oriental charms. Korla Pandit died in California in October 1998. He was survived by his wife and two sons.

All very interesting, but not an exceptional tale, you're probably thinking – and you'd be right. However, the best is yet to come, as the truly interesting part of this story only came to light after his death. In 2001, RJ Smith, editor of the *Los Angeles* magazine, published an article that blew Korla Pandit's ancestry claims out of the water. While he had indeed been born on 16th September 1921, his real name had been John Roland Redd and he had come into the world, not in India, but in St. Louis, Missouri in the United States. His father, Ernest Redd, had been an African-American Baptist pastor and his mother was of Anglo-African ancestry. Consequently, John had comparatively light skin and straight hair, making it relatively easy for him to pass himself off as being of Indian descent. But why the deception?

Being an African American, his opportunities in the early 20th-century United States were severely limited. A colour bar existed at the time, making it virtually impossible for African-American artists to perform. He would not have been allowed to join the Musicians Union and most venues refused to hire African-American performers. To circumvent this bar, John initially adopted the name Juan Rolando and claimed to be Mexican. However, by the 1940s, he and his wife, Beryl, had hit upon the notion of creating the entirely new and exotic persona of Korla Pandit. Beryl designed the make-up and clothing, which included an elaborate turban.

Unlike many performers who choose to use a stage name for professional reasons, Redd had to maintain the persona of Korla Pandit continually in both his public and private life, as to have revealed his true identity to anyone would have risked his entire career and livelihood. Even later in life, when the colour bar no longer existed in the United States, Redd chose not to divulge his true ethnicity. Presumably, he felt that to have done so might have damaged his career, even in those more enlightened times.

Redd kept in touch with his extended family, although he always wore his turban and did not bring his own family with him when making visits. His nephew, Ernest Redd, commented: "Among the family we knew what he was doing and very little was said about it. There was times where he would come by, and it was kind of like a sneak visit. He might come at night sometime and be gone before we got up. He had to separate himself from the family to a certain extent. They would go to see him play, but they wouldn't speak to him. They would go to his show and then they would leave, and the family would greet him at a later time." So successful was his deception that even his sons were not aware of his, or their, African-American heritage.

A documentary about the life of John Roland Redd was released in 2014 entitled *Korla*, which was cast as a classic American story of self-invention. All very well, but it is surely something of an abomination that in the supposed land of the free, he was forced to live a lie just because of his ethnicity.

TWENTY-FOUR

THE MANY LIVES OF STANLEY JACOB WEINBERG

There was nothing about the early life of Stanley Weinberg to suggest that he was destined for a degree of immortality. Born to working-class parents in Brooklyn, New York on 25th November 1890, the young Stanley expressed an interest in a career as a medical doctor. Unfortunately, his parents were unable to pay for the education required to qualify for a career in medicine and so he began his working life as an office clerk. However, Stanley soon became bored of pen-pushing drudgery and so it was not long before he embarked upon a very different career path indeed.

By 1910, Weinberg was working as a United States consul representative to Port du Aubres, near Morocco. Such was his status that he was wined and dined in the finest restaurants New York had to offer. The only trouble was – he wasn't! Journalists, keen to write about the impressive young diplomat, discovered that not only did Port du Aubres not exist, but neither did the position Stanley Weinberg was claiming to have been appointed to. He was arrested for fraud.

Now, one might be forgiven for thinking that having been arrested for impersonating a government official, Weinberg's penchant for imposture would have been severely curtailed – but not a bit of it. For Stanley, this was just the start of a prolific career as an imitator of public figures. Weinberg next put in an appearance as an investigator, working on behalf of the Mayor of New York, until that is the mayor wrote him a stiffly worded letter ordering him to desist from his fraudulent activity. Undeterred, he next claimed to be a decorated bomber pilot, who had fought in the Balkan Wars of 1912–1913.

Stanley was, by now, growing in confidence, and in 1915 he appeared in the guise of a consul general to Romania, using the nom de plume of Ethan Allen Weinberg. Claiming to be acting on a request from the Queen of Romania, he conducted an inspection of the USS *Wyoming*, dressed in a dazzling blue uniform bedecked with gold braid and topped off with an admiral's hat. So convincing was he that he was even given a twenty-one-gun salute on entering New York Harbour. To cap the occasion, Weinberg arranged a sumptuous meal for the ship's officers at the Astor Hotel, the cost of which was to be billed to the Romanian consulate. Unfortunately for Stanley, the banquet resulted in a good deal of publicity and he was, once again, rumbled. On being arrested during the meal, he complained bitterly that the detectives ought to have waited until after dessert. This time, his deception got him a year in jail.

In 1917, he claimed to be a lieutenant in the Army Air Corps by the name of Royal St Cyr and was again arrested, this time while on an inspection of the Brooklyn Armory, when a military tailor grew suspicious owing to irregularities with regard to his uniform. He was again imprisoned for the deception, only this time he remained behind bars until 1920. Upon release, he was soon up to his old tricks and used forged documentation to become a doctor in Lima, Peru, where he lived a lavish lifestyle beyond his means, until his creditors closed in and he was, once again, arrested.

But perhaps his most successful deception occurred in 1921, when Princess Fatima of Afghanistan was visiting the United States, but was struggling to gain official recognition for her visit. Never one to miss an opportunity to deceive, Weinberg called on the princess and claimed to be a State Department liaison officer. Apologising for the oversight, he assured the Afghan royal that he would arrange a meeting with the president. Stanley next visited the State Department and, using the moniker Rodney Stirling Wyman, managed to secure an appointment. On 26th July 1921, Princess Fatima was presented to President Warren G Harding at the White House. On this occasion, his mistake was in posing for photographs with foreign dignitaries. When the photographs appeared in the press, Weinberg was recognised. He was arrested once more and on this occasion was sentenced to two years' imprisonment.

In 1926, Stanley popped up at the funeral of movie

Weinberg on the Left, During the Visit of Princess Fatima to the White House.

star Rudolph Valentino and managed to ingratiate himself with Pola Negri, the actor's grieving fiancée, by claiming to be an eminent doctor. Amazingly, he became her personal physician and issued regular press releases on her condition. He even set up a faith-healing clinic in Valentino's house! Surprisingly, when exposed as a fraud once more, the Polish actress declined to press charges.

On one occasion, Weinberg's ability to deceive was even put to use by the media. The *Evening Graphic* newspaper wanted to secure an interview with Queen Marie of Romania while she was on a visit to the United States, but was not having much luck. Acting on behalf of the publication and purporting to be the Secretary of State, Stanley was granted an audience with the queen and the newspaper subsequently bagged the interview.

Sadly, and somewhat ironically, the end for Stanley Jacob Weinberg came while he was undertaking gainful employment. On 27th August 1960, while working as a night porter at a New York hotel, Stanley confronted an armed robber and was shot dead. The police detective assigned to the case commented: "I've known about the man's past record for years. He did a lot of things in the course of his life, but what he did this time was brave."

The last word is probably best left to Stanley himself and may give a little insight as to his motivation. He once said: "One man's life is a boring thing. I lived many lives: I'm never bored."

TWENTY-FIVE

BITTERSWEET KISS

Frank Hayes loved horses and his ambition in life had always been to be a jockey. Unfortunately for Frank, he grew a bit too much and, at a little over 140 pounds, was just slightly too heavy for the job. Still wanting to work with horses, however, he settled for a career as a trainer and stableman instead. An Irish American, Hayes was born in 1888 and lived in Brooklyn, New York with his mother and sister.

He found employment, initially as a stable hand, with James KL Frayling, a horse breeder, who was quick to spot Frank's potential. Apparently, he had a way with horses and seemed to be able to get the best out of them. Frank Hayes soon gained a reputation as an excellent trainer of thoroughbreds.

A first-class trainer of horses he might have been, but the passion to be a jockey still burned away inside him. However, owing to his size and weight, any horse he rode would have been at a distinct disadvantage and so it seemed that his dream of one day becoming a jockey would never be realised. By the time he was thirty-five years old, Frank had all but resigned himself to a life out of the competitive saddle.

All that was to change, however, at the beginning of June 1923, when Miss AM Frayling, the owner of a horse called Sweet Kiss, which Frank had been training, decided to enter the horse in its first race at a meeting at Belmont Park, New York on 4th June. Owing to the short notice, Miss Frayling was finding it difficult to find a jockey to ride her horse in the race. The fact that Sweet Kiss was a 20/1 outsider may also have played a part in the apparent jockey shortage. Frank immediately saw his chance and offered to ride Miss Frayling's horse in the race. She initially refused his offer, thinking him too heavy, but after promising her that he could lose the required weight in time, she reluctantly agreed to let him ride Sweet Kiss.

Opportunity had finally come knocking and Frank wasn't about to look a gift horse in the mouth (sorry, couldn't resist!) He immediately undertook an intense weight-loss programme and, through a combination of a near starvation diet and rigorous exercise, succeeded in reducing his weight from 142 pounds to 130 pounds in little more than forty-eight hours. He was to ride in the second race of the day – a steeplechase. With the clear favourite being a horse called Gimmie, Sweet Kiss was expected to be little more than an also-ran.

When race day arrived, Frank was ready to take his big chance. Fellow jockeys would later remark on how excited he seemed to be finally making his debut as a jockey. Just before the start, he reportedly turned to the other riders and said, "Today's a good day to make history." How prophetic his comment would come to be.

The steeplechase was to be run over 2 miles and included twelve jumps. The favourite, Gimmie, unsurprisingly took an early lead and continued to lead the charge until the final turn when Sweet Kiss, with Frank in the saddle, unexpectedly moved to the front. With Hayes leaning forward, and seemingly whispering in the horse's ear, they passed the winning post a head in front of Gimmie. Frank had done it. He had won his first race at the age of thirty-five on a 20/1 outsider.

However, as the horse began to slow to a canter, things didn't seem quite right. Miss Frayling and race officials were just preparing to congratulate Frank, who was still leaning forwards in a bizarre manner, when, after about 100 yards, and just as Sweet Kiss was coming to a halt, he fell off. Track physician Dr John Voorhees ran to his aid, but was too late. Frank Hayes was dead!

At some indeterminate point in the race, but thought by witnesses to have been somewhere in the middle, he had suffered a fatal heart attack, believed to have been caused by a combination of his rapid weight

Dead Man Riding.

loss and the excitement of the occasion. Amazingly, the deceased jockey had somehow remained in the saddle even over a number of fences. Astonishingly, Sweet Kiss had won the race with a dead man slumped on her back.

Out of respect for the dead jockey, the race was not contested and post-race formalities were waived, so Belmont's jockey club simply declared him the winner without the traditional weighing-in. Frank Hayes thus became the first, and so far only, person to achieve victory in a competitive sporting engagement post-mortem.

Frank was buried at Holy Cross Cemetery in Brooklyn, New York in the racing silks he had been wearing on that victorious but fateful day.

Unfortunately for Sweet Kiss and her owner, jockeys are a superstitious lot and no one was prepared to ride her thereafter. The horse also gained a new name and was thenceforth known as Sweet Kiss of Death. Miss Frayling was eventually forced to retire the mare, despite boasting an impressive one hundred per cent record of one race, one win.

TWENTY-SIX

A STRANGE ROMANCE

Carl Tanzler was born in Dresden, Germany on 8th February 1877. During his childhood, Tanzler claimed to have had a visitation from a long-dead ancestor, Countess Anna Constantia von Cosel, who purportedly revealed to him the face of his true love – an exotic-looking, dark-haired woman. Notwithstanding the image of the beautiful woman divulged to him in his youth, Carl married Doris Schafer in about 1920, with whom he had two daughters – one of whom sadly died in childhood from diphtheria. In 1926, Tanzler emigrated to the United States and settled in Zephyrhills, Florida, where he was soon joined by his family. However, in 1927, he left his family behind and moved by himself to Key West, Florida, where he found employment at the US Marine Hospital in the capacity of a radiology technician, working in the tuberculosis ward.

It was while at work on 22nd April 1930 that

Carl experienced an epiphanic moment. Worried about the health of her daughter, the mother of Maria Elena Milagro de Hoyos, a local twenty-one-year-old Cuban American, brought her to the hospital for an examination. Tanzler was stunned to recognise her as the beautiful, dark-haired woman from his childhood vision. Despite an age gap of over thirty years, Carl, as his ancestor had predicted, immediately fell in love. Unfortunately, the young woman was subsequently diagnosed with tuberculosis and, despite Tanzler's best efforts to rid her of the disease, died on 25th October 1931.

Not only did the still-obsessed clinical technician pay for Maria's funeral, but he also funded the construction of an above-ground mausoleum in the cemetery at Key West, which he would visit on most nights. Now, you would be forgiven for thinking this behaviour somewhat excessive and possibly even unhealthy, but what he did next took things to a whole other level. One night in April 1933, Tanzler slipped, unnoticed, through the gates of the cemetery and removed the body of the dead woman from her mausoleum, wheeling it through the darkness on a toy wagon all the way to his home. He later claimed that Maria's spirit would often come to him during his nocturnal visits to her tomb and implore him to take her from her resting place.

Carl Tanzler in 1940.

At his home, he set about reconstructing the corpse from

the decomposing remains. He used wire and coat hangers to reattach the bones, fitted the sockets with glass eyes and fashioned a wig from her hair. He replaced the decomposing skin with silk cloth soaked in plaster of Paris and wax and filled the torso with rags to re-establish the woman's original body shape. He dressed the cadaver in stockings, gloves and jewellery and placed the macabre restoration in his bed. As you might imagine, vast quantities of perfume, air-fresheners, disinfectants and preserving agents were also required to combat the smell and speed of decomposition.

In 1940, following a report that Tanzler had been seen dancing in front of an open window with what appeared to be a corpse, Maria's sister became suspicious and notified the authorities. When the mausoleum was duly opened and found to be bereft of a body, the distraught woman immediately knew where she would find her dead sister. On arriving at Tanzler's house, she was invited inside and was horrified to discover what looked like a waxwork of her deceased sibling lying in bed. He calmly explained that he and Maria were in love and very happy together and even invited her to pay them a return visit. She instead visited the police, who quickly arrived at the house and took the weird remains to the local morgue for an autopsy.

As if things were not already disturbing enough,

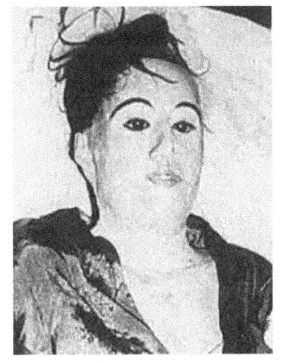

Maria Elena Milagro de Hoyos in Life and Death.

the autopsy was to reveal one more repulsive fact. Two physicians, Dr DePoo and Dr Foraker, who were present at the pathological examination, revealed that a tube had been inserted into the vaginal area of the corpse, permitting sexual intercourse with the deceased woman. It appeared that Carl Tanzler had been engaging in acts of necrophilia for as much as seven years. Following the autopsy, the body was, for some reason, put on display at a local funeral home, where it was viewed by almost 7000 people. Eventually, it was returned to Key West Cemetery, although this time it was buried secretly in an unmarked grave to prevent any further intervention by Tanzler.

Carl Tanzler was arrested and remanded in custody. After being found mentally competent following a psychiatric examination, he was charged with 'wantonly and maliciously destroying a grave and removing a body without permission'. However, owing to the length of time that had elapsed since the incident of grave robbing, the authorities were unable to proceed with the case against him as the statute of limitations for the crime had expired. Oddly, the public attitude towards Tanzler was surprisingly sympathetic, with many simply regarding him as an eccentric romantic.

In 1944, Tanzler moved to Pasco County, Florida, close to Zephyrhills, where his wife still lived. Apparently, she helped to support him in his later years. His obsession with the dead woman, however, lingered on. He used a death mask of Maria to create a life-sized effigy, which he lived with until his death. Carl Tanzler died at home on approximately 3rd July 1952, although his body was not discovered until about three weeks after his death. Rumours quickly circulated that the effigy was, in fact, the real body of Maria and that he had somehow managed to switch them. A strange romance, indeed!

TWENTY-SEVEN

THE MEN FROM NOWHERE

On a warm day in July 1954, immigration officials at Tokyo's Haneda Airport in Japan were busy processing international arrivals, when an officer checking passports noticed something odd. When a bearded, light-skinned businessman handed over his passport to be stamped, the officer was perplexed to observe that his passport had been issued from a country called Taured. After checking with a colleague, who confirmed that no such country existed, it was determined that the man should be held for further investigation. Apparently, the passport looked like an authentic document and bore the stamps of many airports around the world, including evidence of previous trips to Tokyo.

His principal language appeared to be French, although he also spoke Japanese sufficiently well for the authorities to be able to interrogate him without an interpreter. When questioned, the man was brazenly insistent that Taured really did exist, pointing out

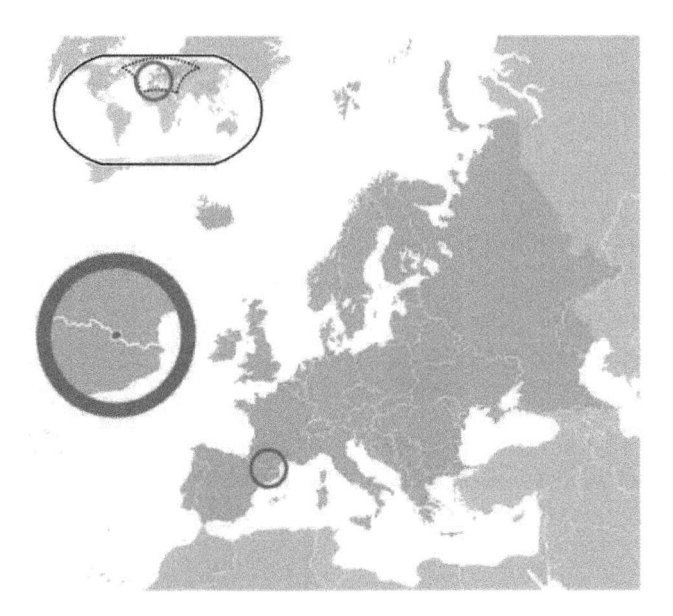

Andorra is Indeed Located Between France and Spain.

that it had been a recognised country for the last one thousand years. He explained that it was located between France and Spain and, when shown a map, immediately pointed to the Principality of Andorra, questioning why the map was misrepresenting his country of origin. There followed something of a Mexican stand-off, with Japanese officials insisting that Taured did not exist and the strange traveller insisting that it did.

With things at something of an impasse, it was decided to detain the man overnight at a local hotel, in order to give the immigration department more time to look into the mysterious matter. With the aim of preventing him from leaving without permission, he was assigned a room several floors up with no balcony and two guards were placed outside the door. Among the man's possessions, they found a considerable amount of cash in various European currencies and documentation relating to his employment. When officials contacted his employer, however, they claimed never to have heard of the individual in question. Additionally, the company he claimed he was visiting in Tokyo to do business with also denied any knowledge of him, and it was the same story with the hotel where he insisted he had made a reservation.

The Japanese were, by now, growing increasingly suspicious of their puzzling guest and determined to get to the bottom of the mystery. However, when officials arrived the following morning to bring him back for further questioning, they found his room vacant. The enigmatic man had simply vanished, along with all his personal effects.

A strange and perplexing tale without parallel, you may be forgiven for thinking. I certainly was. It turns out, however, that there are other such stories of travellers claiming to originate from non-existent countries. In the spring of 1851, a man arrived at a small village near Frankfurt an der Oder, Germany. He was fair-skinned and spoke only a little German. He claimed that his name was Jophar Vorin and that he hailed from a country called Laxaria, in the continent of Sakria. Other than a smattering of German, he did not appear to understand any other European language. He stated that he had set out on his journey in order to search for a long-lost brother, but that he had been shipwrecked along the way, although when shown a map he was unable to identify where he had come from or the route he had taken.

He explained that he was fluent in both Laxarian and Abramian, the former being the language of his common countryfolk and the latter being a more formal written language used by priestly orders. His religion was called Ispatian, the doctrine of which appeared to be Christian in form. He maintained that the earth contained five great continents called Sakria, Aflar, Astar, Auslar and Euplar, and that his home country of Laxaria was many hundreds of miles away across a vast ocean. The burgomaster of Frankfurt an der Oder was so perplexed by the man's story that he had him sent to Berlin, the nation's capital, in order that his fantastical claims could be properly investigated by government officials. Unfortunately, there does not appear to be any written record of what happened to him after that. Perhaps, like the man from Taured, he simply disappeared!

Another case occurred in 1905, this time in Paris, France, where a man was apprehended for stealing bread. When interviewed, he could speak only a completely unrecognisable language and claimed to be from a place called Lizbia. Assuming he meant Lisbon, the capital of Portugal, he was shown a map, but displayed no recognition when Portugal was pointed out to him.

So, what are we to make of these implausible stories? The most straightforward answer is that they are simply urban legends and are not actually true. The fact that we do not have a name for the man from Taured nor a conclusion to the story of the man from Laxaria certainly adds weight to the urban myth hypothesis. But should we just dismiss them as the products of over-fertile imaginations? As with my earlier story, 'The Strange Double Life of Emilie Sagee', there exists another intriguing possible explanation for these perplexing outliers and, surprisingly, it comes to us from the world of quantum physics. Quantum physics – or quantum mechanics, as it is sometimes referred to – is the study of nature at atomic and subatomic levels, and suggests the possibility of multiple dimensions. Might our weary travellers have inadvertently transgressed the dimensional veil and unintentionally arrived in another existence, just for a while?

TWENTY-EIGHT

THE MYSTERIOUS DEATH OF ELISA LAM AT THE CECIL HOTEL

The Cecil Hotel was opened in 1927 on Main Street, Los Angeles, California in the United States. It has 600 rooms and originally targeted the business traveller and tourist market. However, despite being regarded as a fashionable destination for a number of decades, it had, by the end of the 1940s, been overshadowed by more glamorous hotels in upmarket parts of the city. Notwithstanding the fluctuating fortunes of the establishment, however, it is the hotel's reputation for murder and mystery that makes it noteworthy.

At approximately 10am on the morning of 15th January 1947, local resident Betty Bersinger was out walking with her three-year-old daughter, when she came upon what she initially thought was a discarded shop mannequin. To her horror, she quickly realised that what she was actually looking at was the mutilated body of a young woman. The corpse had been severed in two at the waist, disfigured and drained of blood. The killer had also carved a grotesque smile on the woman's face from ear to ear. The body was identified as that of twenty-two-year-old aspiring actress Elizabeth Short. The last known sighting of Elizabeth prior to her death had been at the bar of the Cecil Hotel. The case remains one of America's most brutal, unsolved murders.

Elizabeth Short.

In 1964, a long-term resident of the hotel, known as 'Pigeon Goldie' Osgood, was murdered in her room. She had been raped, beaten and stabbed. This case also remains unsolved. A number of suicides also occurred at the Cecil, leading to it being given the unwanted nickname, 'The Suicide'. Serial killers also feature in the chequered history of the hotel. Richard Ramirez, aka the 'Night Stalker', resided at the Cecil in the mid-1980s, during which time he is thought to have murdered up to thirteen people. Jack Unterweger was also staying there in 1991 when he murdered three prostitutes.

But undoubtedly, the most bizarre death at the Cecil Hotel occurred much more recently. In February 2013, twenty-one-year-old Canadian student Elisa Lam was recorded on the hotel elevator's surveillance camera behaving erratically. She entered the elevator and pressed numerous buttons. Perhaps confused by so many conflicting instructions, the elevator stayed put with the door open. She appeared agitated, glancing out of the door as if expecting, or trying to hide from, someone. She exited and re-entered the elevator a couple of times, before standing just outside the elevator door and making weird, unnatural gesticulations with her arms and hands. Finally, she walks away. Footage of the recording can be viewed on YouTube by simply searching for 'Elisa Lam'. The clip is just under four minutes in length.

Two weeks later, guests at the hotel began complaining of foul-tasting water. The water tower on the roof of the building was inspected and the naked, decomposing body of Elisa was found floating therein. Her personal effects were also found in the water. There was no evidence of drug consumption and Elisa left no suicide note, leading the Los Angeles County coroner to rule her death as accidental drowning, also noting that she was possibly suffering from bipolar disorder. However, the ruling of the death of Elisa Lam as accidental, raises more questions than it answers. Firstly, the door to the roof was locked and alarmed, so Elisa ought not to have been able to gain access to the roof area. Secondly, the water tower was high and could only have been accessed via a ladder. There was no ladder on the roof. Also, gaining access to the tower required considerable strength and Elisa was just 5 feet 5 inches tall and weighed only 121 pounds.

Odd circumstances, indeed. But there was more strangeness to come, leading some to assign a paranormal explanation to the death. Elisa's phone was never recovered, but her Tumblr account mysteriously started posting images and continued to do so for six months after her death. Also, a bizarre coincidence concerned an outbreak of tuberculosis, which occurred near to the hotel shortly after the discovery of her body. The testing kit used in such outbreaks is, astonishingly, named 'LAM-ELISA'.

Another strange coincidence relates to a horror movie released in 2005 called *Dark Waters*. It is the story of a young woman who drowns in the water tank atop an apartment building. Her body remains undiscovered for some time and begins to decompose, and she is only found after residents begin to complain of foul-tasting water. The mirroring of the tragic story of Elisa Lam eight years later is perplexing. An example of precognition on the part of the writers, perhaps.

Coincidence or synchronicity? Precognition? Is a supernatural entity trying to tell us something? Did Elisa Lam drown accidentally or commit suicide? Or was she murdered by someone or *something*? I don't know, but I think I'll give the Cecil Hotel a miss.

TWENTY-NINE

PORKY BICKAR AND THE MOUNT EDGECUMBE ERUPTION

The eruption of Mount Edgecumbe – located at the southern end of Kruzof Island, Alaska – in April 1974 may not be up there with the likes of Krakatoa, which burst forth in 1883, or Mount Tambora, which blew its top in 1815, or even Mount St Helens, which resulted in the US's most deadly volcanic event when it let rip in May 1980, but it nevertheless deserves its place in history, albeit for a very different reason to the more destructive events mentioned above.

Mount Edgecumbe lies about 10 miles east of the Queen Charlotte Fault, which separates the North American and Pacific Plates, and, at 3201 feet, is the highest point in the Mount Edgecumbe volcanic field. The mountain had originally been called L'ux by the indigenous Tlingit people, who considered it sacred. However, it was Captain James Cook who gave it its current name, when he came upon it on 2nd May 1778 – most likely after Mount Edgecumbe, a hill that overlooks Plymouth Harbour in the southwest of England.

The first recorded ascent of Mount Edgecumbe was that made by Captain Urey Lisanski of the Imperial Russian Navy in July 1805, but by the 1930s a trail to the top of the mountain had been established. For those who enjoy an energetic hike, the trail is approximately 6.8 miles in length, with the ascent becoming steep before ending above the treeline in a barren landscape of volcanic ash and snow at about 2000 feet. From there, signposts direct hikers onwards and upwards towards the rim of the caldera.

Oliver 'Porky' Bickar was born on 1st November 1923 in Chehalis, Washington in the United States and fought in World War II, taking part in the D-Day invasion of Normandy, France. After the war, he married Patricia (Patty) in 1950 and they had three children. In 1960, the family moved to Sitka, Alaska,

The Eruption of Mount Edgecumbe – Harold Wahlman, 1st April 1974.

where Porky worked in the logging industry. In 1964, he set up his own business, Porky's Equipment Inc., which sold and serviced logging gear. He was well known in the area and gained a degree of notoriety for his annual performance at the All-Alaska Logging Championships, where he would fell a tree with such precision that it would hit a predetermined target on the ground. Porky was also an artist who worked in metal, producing cut-outs of the local fauna, which he displayed in public locations around the town.

All fine and dandy, you're probably thinking, but what the heck has old Porky got to do with the eruption of Mount Edgecumbe in 1974? Well, a lot, as it happens. You see, there are a couple of things I neglected to mention. Firstly, Mount Edgecumbe is a dormant volcano that last erupted over 4000 years ago. Secondly, the eruption in 1974 took place on 1st April – or April Fool's Day, as it is alternatively known. Yes, you've guessed it, Porky was also a prankster. Previous pranks included blocking a friend's driveway with a felled tree and putting plastic flamingos in trees to confuse tourists on wildlife boat trips. His finest achievement as a practitioner of mischievousness, however, occurred on 1st April 1974, when, for a short while, he tricked the world into thinking the dormant Mount Edgecumbe had erupted once more.

So, how did he do it? Well, the wheeze first occurred to Porky in 1971, but he had to wait patiently for three years before favourable weather conditions meant that the summit would be visible from a considerable distance on April Fool's Day. Finally, on 1st April 1974, the weather was just right. He had, in the intervening time, amassed a collection of approximately seventy old tyres, which he stored in an aircraft hangar. Waking that morning, he peered out of the window and, able to see Mount Edgecumbe clearly in the distance, announced to his wife, "I have to go do it today." She was reported to have replied: "Just don't make an ass of yourself."

Initially, Porky ran into a spot of bother. He needed to arrange for the tyres to be transported to the top of the mountain, but, to his consternation, the first two helicopter pilots he contacted refused to take on the task. Fortunately, it was third time lucky and a pilot by the name of Earl Walker agreed to help out with the caper. Having secured the services of a helicopter and pilot, he piled the tyres into canvas slings, which were hooked onto the underside of the helicopter. With the addition of smoke bombs and several gallons of kerosene, they headed off to the crater. Having piled the combustible material into the caldera of the dormant

Porky Bickar in 1991.

volcano, Porky stomped the words 'APRIL FOOL' in the snow nearby, before setting the assemblage alight and heading for home.

So successful was the prank that the Associated Press got hold of the story and it ran in newspapers around the world. When Mount St Helens actually erupted in 1980, Porky received a communication from an attorney in Denver. Inside, the envelope was a photograph of the erupting volcano with a note attached that read: 'This time, you little bastard, you've gone too far.' Porky was rightly proud of his achievement, writing: 'On April Fool's Day, I hired a chopper and flew 70 old, kerosene-soaked tyres on top of the dormant volcano, Mt. Edgecumbe, that looms over Sitka. I set the tyres on fire, and the billowing black smoke created one hell of a commotion in Sitka. I dare you to top that April Fools' joke.'

Oliver 'Porky' Bickar died on 11th August 2003 at the age of seventy-nine and is buried in Sitka National Cemetery. Nice one, Porky!

THIRTY

THE SCIENCE OF LAZARUS

To refer to Robert E Cornish as a scientific child prodigy would be a slight exaggeration, but only just. Born in San Francisco, California, United States in 1903, he had completed high school by the age of fifteen and went on to graduate from Berkley just three years later. By the age of twenty-one, he was a practising physician. His true passion, however, was research and so it was that in his mid-twenties he returned to Berkley to immerse himself once more in the world of academia. Projects he engaged in ranged from objective experimentation, such as the isolation of heavy water, to rather eccentric notions, such as the development of special lenses to enable newspapers to be read underwater.

Cornish was widely regarded as an exceptional talent, occasionally given over to idiosyncratic tendencies. However, young Robert was soon to earn himself a degree of notoriety, owing to a macabre obsession with death, or rather with its reversal. Yes, Cornish had decided to turn his extensive abilities to the not inconsiderable task of bringing the dead back to life. Not since Jesus Christ supposedly performed a miracle approximately 2000 years ago, raising a man named Lazarus from the dead, is this feat believed to have been achieved. I think I would have stuck to underwater lenses myself.

Doctor Robert E Cornish.

His process of reanimating the deceased involved the use of a teeterboard, which, while not unlike a two-person see-saw, involved only one participant – a dead one. In 1933, Cornish somehow managed to get hold of an unspecified number of human cadavers, which he would strap to the teeterboard, inject with adrenaline and heparin, and then vigorously teeter them back and forth in order to restore circulation. It didn't work. However, Robert was undeterred, blaming the failures on the fact that his 'patients' had been dead for too long to enable resurrection to take place.

He needed fresh corpses. Finding very recently deceased humans in short supply, Cornish turned his attention to dogs in 1934. So confident was he that he could bring dead dogs back to life, he organised a public demonstration. He duly arrived with five fox terriers in tow, each of which he had named Lazarus, after the corpse successfully reinvigorated by Jesus. Disconcertingly, he then proceeded to euthanise each of the dogs, much to the discomfort and consternation of most of the onlookers. After the poor animals had been dead for five minutes, he initiated his process of resurrection. They were strapped to the teeterboard, injected with a concoction of chemicals and robustly rocked back and forth. Three of the dogs steadfastly refused to return from the afterlife, presumably preferring doggy heaven to being experimented on by a slightly unhinged doctor.

However, to the amazement of those present, two of the dogs were successfully restored to life. In one case, the success was only partial, with the pitiful canine in a kind of vegetative state, apparently blind, unresponsive and able only to wander about zombie-like, with no indication that it was even aware of its surroundings. The fifth dog, however, was a different story. Initially, it appeared also to have been reanimated to a zombified state, but it gradually recovered its faculties and returned to normal. Given that Robert Cornish demonstrated that he could indeed bring the dead back to life, his public experiment was considered to have been a remarkable success.

While the unconventional doctor believed himself to be something of a pioneer in the field of reanimation of the dead, others were significantly less impressed. Many people expressed outrage at the killing of dogs for experimentation purposes, while others questioned the purpose of it all. He began to be regarded as something of a Dr Frankenstein figure by the general public and found himself ostracised by his colleagues, even losing his job as a consequence. Undeterred by the criticism, however, Cornish was adamant that his procedure would work on humans and, in 1947, announced that he intended to carry out the resuscitation of a freshly deceased corpse, by applying his methodology to a prisoner who had just been executed by the state.

A report contemporaneous with his announcement went as follows: 'Dr Cornish, elated at the sensational success of his experiments with dogs, wants to make the attempt on humans. He is now seeking permission to experiment with a criminal executed by poison gas. Given the body after physicians declare the man to be dead, he would strap the body to a teeterboard and attach electrical heating pads to the limbs. Next, a chemical known as methylene blue would be injected into the veins to neutralise the poisonous fumes that had caused death. Pure oxygen would then be pumped into the lungs through a mask and the teeterboard rocked slowly to keep the blood in circulation... Dr Cornish believes firmly that the dead man would live. He does not agree with other scientists that the brain of the man so revived would be hopelessly damaged.'

Hearing of Cornish's proposal, a convicted child killer named Thomas McMonigle, who was on death row awaiting execution at San Quentin State Prison, reached out to the resurrectionist doctor to volunteer to be the subject of his experiment. After all, what had he got to lose? Cornish approached the California Department of Corrections for permission to carry out his procedure on the body of McGonigle, but his request was refused. Not only would such an attempt have been unethical, but they would have faced an additional problem had he succeeded. McMonigle, having been executed, would have technically served his sentence and would have had to be freed. In addition, he would have been protected by the law of double jeopardy, which prevented a person from being tried for the same crime twice. Thus, the authorities would have had no option but to free a convicted child killer with no prospect of being able to rearrest him. Thomas McMonigle was executed on 20th February 1948 and with Cornish having been denied permission to intervene, he remained very dead indeed.

Having failed to obtain the necessary authorisation for his macabre experimentation, Cornish faded into obscurity, reduced to earning a living marketing his own product: 'Dr Cornish's Tooth Powder with Vitamin D and Fluoride'. Robert E Cornish himself died on 6th March 1963 at the age of sixty, taking his life-restoring secrets with him into the afterlife. Was he just a mad scientist or had he really discovered a way of defeating death? What would have happened had he been allowed to try and revive McMonigle? Unless someone else takes up his resurrectionist baton, we are unlikely ever to know – probably just as well.

THIRTY-ONE

THE WHIMSICAL HORACE DE VERE COLE

The English upper class has for centuries been littered with eccentric individuals whose unconventional behaviour has left the more rationally minded bemused. Whether this is due to generations of inbreeding or simply the result of boredom caused by having too much leisure time remains a matter for conjecture. Whatever the reason for their outlandish behaviour, there is surely no better example of the genre than Horace de Vere Cole, who seems to have stepped straight out of the pages of a PG Wodehouse novel, although even Bertie Wooster would surely have regarded his conduct as beyond the pale. A classic example of truth being stranger than fiction.

Horace was born on 5th May 1881 in Ballincollig, County Cork, Ireland. His mother, Mary de Vere, was heiress of Sir Stephen de Vere and related to the de Vere Earls of Oxford. In addition, his paternal

Horace de Vere Cole.

grandfather had made a fortune dealing in quinine, a chemical used in the treatment of malaria and also an ingredient of tonic water. However, it is not for his privileged family background that he is primarily remembered today. Horace de Vere Cole was to take the art of pranking to a whole other level and, in so doing, cement his place in the hierarchy of English upper-class eccentrics.

His first recorded prank occurred while he was an undergraduate at Cambridge. In March 1905, on learning that the Sultan of Zanzibar was visiting London, Cole sent a telegram to the Mayor of Cambridge, informing him that the Sultan's uncle and entourage had decided to pay a visit to the famous university city and asking him to show them around. Horace and his friend, Adrian Stephen (the brother of author Virginia Woolf), dressed up in robes and turbans and applied heavy make-up in order to appear of African origin. The mayor and town clerk duly provided the imposters with a reception followed by a comprehensive tour of the university, before returning them to the train station in order for them to make their journey back to London. The pair apparently boarded the train, but then alighted a few carriages down and simply left through a side exit of the station.

However, Horace de Vere Cole is best remembered

for a prank that became known as the Dreadnought hoax. In the early 20th century, HMS *Dreadnought* was the most powerful and technologically advanced battleship afloat and was understandably the pride of the British Royal Navy. On 7th February 1910, Cole, along with Virginia Woolf, Adrian Stephen, Guy Ridley, Anthony Buxton and Duncan Grant, carried out a deception that was so successful, it caused a minor sensation at the time and left the naval hierarchy severely embarrassed. Woolf, Grant, Buxton and Ridley donned robes and turbans, and applied skin darkening make-up and fake beards, in order to impersonate members of the Abyssinian royal family. Stephen and Cole remained in western attire, with the former acting as interpreter and the latter claiming to be 'Herbert Cholmondeley' of the Foreign Office.

At Paddington Station in London, the party was given a VIP coach for the train journey to Weymouth, from where they were taken directly to HMS *Dreadnought*. They were welcomed with an honour guard, although as an Abyssinian flag could not be found, the navy decided to use the flag of Zanzibar instead and the band played the Zanzibar national anthem. The group inspected the fleet and bestowed fake military honours on a number of officers. Since none of the imposters were familiar with the various languages spoken by Abyssinians, they spoke in gibberish, using words and phrases they had learned from Greek and Latin, and, when expressing delight, enthusiastically declared, "Bunga Bunga". Unfortunately, the party was unable to accept the offer of a celebratory meal, as they were concerned that the act of chewing would cause their fake beards to fall off.

The Dreadnought Hoaxers.

When the prank was revealed, the navy demanded the arrest of Cole as ringleader. However, as he had not broken any law, the authorities were powerless to act. Thereafter, it was not uncommon for members of the public to shout, "Bunga Bunga!" when spotting a naval officer in the street. In 1915, during World War I, HMS *Dreadnought* sank a German submarine. Among the congratulatory telegrams was one that simply read: 'Bunga Bunga'.

While on honeymoon in Italy, Cole deposited piles of horse manure in Venice, which caused much consternation among the locals, not least because there were no horses in the city and it could only be reached by boat. On another occasion in London, Cole challenged Member of Parliament Oliver Locker-Lampson to a running race, with Cole so confident of victory that he gave the MP a 10-yard head start. However, he had slipped his gold watch into Locker-Lampson's pocket and, as the sprinting pair approached a policeman, Cole began shouting, "Stop, thief!" The unfortunate politician was immediately arrested, although he was released without charge when the prank was revealed. Cole, on the other hand, was fined £5 for breaching the peace.

As a theatre critic, he came up with a unique way of expressing his displeasure. Reacting to a play he considered pretentious, he purchased eight tickets with predetermined seat numbers for a performance and gave the tickets to eight bald men, who each had a letter painted on their heads. When they took their seats, the word 'BOLLOCKS' was clearly visible to audience members in the circle and stalls. On another occasion, he hosted a party with carefully selected guests. As the evening progressed, it became apparent to all in attendance that every single guest had the word 'bottom' in their surname.

Without doubt, though, his most shocking prank was one that he repeated on numerous occasions. He would wander along a busy street with a cow's udder protruding from the fly of his trousers. When confronted, he would apologise profusely, whip out a pair of scissors and cut-off the offending appendage. The reaction of those who witnessed this apparent act of self-mutilation has sadly been lost to history.

Horace de Vere Cole was twice married and died of a heart attack in 1936, aged just fifty-four. His sister was the wife of Prime Minister Neville Chamberlain, who once said of his brother-in-law, "I think he must be a little mad". Quite!

THIRTY-TWO

JACOB MILLER'S TOUGH NUT

Jacob Miller was a soldier in the Union Army that fought against the Confederacy in the American Civil War. On 19th September 1863, during the Battle of Chickamauga, he was shot in the forehead. Given the rudimentary medical care available in the mid-19th century and the lack of facilities on hand, this should have been the end of poor Jacob. However, it seems that the young soldier had other ideas. What happened next was described by Miller in his own words:

> "When I came to my senses sometime after, I found I was in the rear of the confederate line. So not to become a prisoner, I made up my mind to make an effort to get around their line and back on my own side. I got up with the help of my gun as a staff, then went back some distance, then started parallel with the line of battle. I suppose I was so

covered with blood that those that I met, did not notice that I was a Yank (at least our Major, my former captain did not recognize me when I met him after passing to our own side). By this time, my head was swelled so bad it shut my eyes and I could see to get along only by raising the lid of my right eye with my finger and looking ahead, then going on till I ran afoul of something, then would look again and so on."

Eventually, exhausted from his toils, he laid down by the side of the road. Fortunately, some passing stretcher-bearers saw him, put him on a stretcher and carried him to the field hospital.

"A hospital nurse came and put a wet bandage over my wound and around my head and gave me a canteen of water. The surgeons examined my wound and decided it was best not to operate on me and give me more pain as they said I couldn't live very long, so the nurse took me back into the tent. I slept some during the night. The next morning, the doctors came around to make a list of the wounded and said they were sending all the wounded to Chattanooga, Tennessee. But they told me I was wounded too bad to be moved."

Fearing that he would be taken prisoner by the Confederates if he were left behind, Jacob decided to take matters into his own hands.

"I made up my mind, as long as I could, to drag one foot after another. I got a nurse to fill my canteen with water so I could make an effort in getting as near to safety as possible. I got out of the tent without being noticed and got behind some wagons that stood near the road till I was safely away – having to open my eye with my finger to take my bearings on the road. I went away from the boom of cannon and the rattle of musketry. I worked my way along the road as best I could. At one time, I got off to the side of the road and bumped my head against a low hanging limb. The shock toppled me over, I got up and took my bearings again and went on as long as I could drag a foot, then lay down beside the road."

Once again, fortune was on Jacob's side. The wagons of wounded heading for Chattanooga began to pass by.

"One of the drivers asked if I was alive and said he would take me in, as one of his men had died back aways, and he had taken him out."

Once inside, he passed out. Upon waking, Jacob found himself in Chattanooga.

"[I was] lying with hundreds of other wounded on the floor almost as thick as hogs in a stock car. Some were talking, some were groaning. I raised myself to a sitting position, got my canteen and wet my head. While doing it, I heard a couple of soldiers who were from my company. They could not believe it was me as they said I was left for dead on the field. They came over to where I was, and we visited together till an order came for all the wounded that could walk to start across the river on a pontoon bridge to a hospital. We were to be treated and taken to Nashville. I told the boys if they could lead me, I could walk that distance.

When we arrived across, we found our company teamster, who we stopped with that night. He got us something to eat. It was the first thing I had tasted since Saturday morning, two days earlier. After we ate, we lay down on a pile of blankets, each fixed under the wagon and rested pretty well as the teamsters stayed awake till nearly morning to keep our wounds moist with cool water from a nearby spring. The next morning, we awoke to the crackling of the campfire. We got a cup of coffee and a bite of hard tack and fat meat to eat. While eating, an orderly rode up and asked if we were wounded. If so, we were to go back along the road to get our wounds dressed, so we bid the teamsters good-bye and went to get our wounds attended to. That was the first time my wound was washed and dressed by a surgeon."

Shortly thereafter, the wounded were sent to Bridgeport, Alabama, by wagon.

"The jolting hurt my head so badly I could not stand it, so I had to get out. My comrades got out with me, and we went on foot."

Astonishingly, given his condition, he walked the 60 miles to Bridgeport in four days. During the journey, Jacob was finally able to open his right eye without using his fingers. From Bridgeport, they caught a train to Nashville. So exhausted was Jacob by this time, that he passed out during the ride. When Jacob eventually regained consciousness, he found himself sitting in a tub of warm water in a hospital in Nashville. From there, he was transferred to a hospital in Louisville, Kentucky and then onto yet another in New Albany, Indiana. Jacob desperately wanted the bullet to be removed.

Jacob Miller in His Later Years.

> "In all the hospitals I was in, I begged the surgeons to operate on my head, but they all refused."

After nine months of suffering, Jacob finally found two doctors who agreed to operate on his wound. They removed the musket ball and he remained in hospital until he was de-enlisted on 17th September 1864, almost one year after being shot. However, it seems that the doctors failed to remove all of the foreign debris from Jacob's head.

> "Seventeen years after I was wounded, a buck shot dropped out of my wound. And thirty one years after, two pieces of lead came out."

Many years later, when asked how he could recall the matter in such detail, he replied, "I have an everyday reminder of it in my wound and constant pain in the head, never free of it while not asleep. The whole scene is imprinted on my brain as with a steel engraving." However, Jacob was not one to complain, commenting, "The government is good to me and give me $40 per month pension."

The above account is taken from an interview he gave to *The Joliet Daily News*, who published his remarkable story on 14th June 1911, almost fifty years after he sustained, what should have been, his fatal injury. Jacob Miller died in about 1917, aged approximately seventy-five. Not bad going for a man who spent around half a century with lead in his head.

THIRTY-THREE

THE SIN-EATERS

During the course of the Middle Ages, the grim reaper was a far more frequent visitor than today. Illness, famine and pestilence were commonplace and, with a medical knowledge based on the theories of the ancients, treatments were largely ineffectual and, as a consequence, little could be done to alleviate suffering. However, it was not just the fear of death that struck dread into the medieval heart. What was to become of their soul? Europe in the Middle Ages was a place of almost universal religious belief and the notion that one's soul, in order to atone for mortal sins, might arrive in purgatory or, worse still, be damned to hell for eternity terrified those who found themselves approaching their demise, after a lifetime of less-than-pious observance of God's will.

So, what was to be done? For the wealthy, who, at the time, consisted of the nobility and landed gentry, no problem. As death approached, the expiring individual or their family could pay a member of the clergy, preferably a bishop, to absolve the rapidly declining man or woman of their sins, thus ensuring a smooth passage of the soul into a heavenly afterlife at the appropriate juncture. However, the vast majority of the population at the time were far from wealthy and most lived by subsistence farming, meaning they ate what they grew with little else to show for their labours. Indeed, a percentage of their crops even had to be paid to the lord of the manor in the form of a tythe, meaning the rich grew richer and the poor, poorer. So what options were available to the peasant class with regard to the redemption of the soul?

Fortunately, all was not lost. For the price of a few pennies and a little food and drink, the family of a recently deceased villein or serf could call upon the services of a sin-eater. An odd job title, no doubt, but one that is, nevertheless, relatively self-explanatory. The duties of a sin-eater obliged them to visit the home of the just departed and partake of nourishment, usually in the form of ale and bread. Typically, the beer would

Sin-Eating.

be placed next to the corpse and the bread on its chest. By consuming the frugal meal, the sins of the dead individual would be absorbed into the sin-eater, thus absolving them of their sins and, as with their wealthy counterparts, ensuring that they would be welcomed into the Kingdom of Heaven. Just before eating the food, the sin-eater would utter an incantation that went as follows: "I give easement and rest now to thee, dear man. Come not down the lanes or in our meadows. And for thy peace, I pawn my own soul. Amen."

While the services of sin-eaters were regarded as almost a rite of passage for successful entry into the afterlife, the lot of the sin-eater was not a happy one. Believing sin-eaters to become more depraved each time they gobbled up the sins of the departed, they were viewed as the epitome of immorality and ungodliness. Consequently, their services were procured surreptitiously, with the sin-eater usually being obliged to call round covertly after dark. They were shunned by society and reviled like lepers, so lived on the outskirts of the communities they served. As you might imagine, the profession tended to attract only the most wretched and impoverished of individuals who, but for the meagre rations and small change, might otherwise have starved to death. Interestingly, it seems that when a sin-eater died, it was customary for another, often younger, sin-eater to perform the sin-eating ritual over the corpse of his or her deceased colleague, thus absolving the deceased sin-eater of their multitude of sins.

Rather surprisingly, the practice of sin-eating seems to have persisted into relatively modern times, only dying out in the 19th century. In 1825, a Professor

Evans of the Presbyterian College, Carmarthen, Wales described a sin-eater he had met as follows: 'Abhorred by the superstitious villagers as a thing unclean, the sin-eater cut himself off from all social intercourse with his fellow creatures by reason of the life he had chosen; he lived as a rule in a remote place by himself, and those who chanced to meet him avoided him as they would a leper. This unfortunate was held to be the associate of evil spirits, and given to witchcraft, incantations, and unholy practices; only when a death took place did they seek him out, and when his purpose was accomplished they burned the wooden bowl and platter from which he had eaten the food handed across, or placed on the corpse for his consumption.'

Indeed, the last-known sin-eater in England was a man named Richard Munslow, who died on 23rd April 1906 aged approximately seventy-four. However, by the time Richard took up the profession, it appears that the jobholder may not have been quite as reviled and impoverished as his predecessors. He married Ann Pinches on 14th January 1862 at Ratlinghope parish church and they had seven children. When he passed away, Richard Munslow was buried with an impressive headstone in the churchyard of St Margaret's, Ratlinghope, Shropshire, England. His grave can be viewed today and his tombstone was actually restored following a public subscription. A special service to commemorate the restoration was held at the

The Grave of Richard Munslow.

graveside on Sunday 19th September 2010. However, the death of Richard Munslow begs the question that must surely have bothered him and his family. Who eats the last sin-eater's sins?

THIRTY-FOUR

THE AMAZING VICTORIAN MACHINE OF DEATH

On a Sunday morning on 11th June 1876, a police officer had just popped into a hotel in Lafayette, Indiana, United States, called the Lahr House, for refreshment, when a chambermaid, pale and breathless, suddenly interrupted his repose. The young lady had been attending to her duties, cleaning and servicing the hotel's guest rooms, when she made a gruesome discovery in room 41. The officer, along with a number of members of staff, quickly made their way to the room and were greeted with an unforgettable sight. The headless body of a man was strapped to the floor, encircled by a copious amount of blood, and the severed head lay in a box partly filled with cotton wool.

The initial assumption that the chambermaid had stumbled upon a murder scene was quickly ruled out, as the room also contained a remarkable contraption bearing the words: 'Karikari. Patent applied for'. So, what was this strange mechanical device and what did it do? As you may have guessed, it had everything to do with the parting of the man's head from body. The mechanism consisted of a broad axe, which had been sharpened to a razor's edge, attached to two heavy iron bars to give added weight. The handle of the axe was attached to a beam in such a manner as enabled it to rotate and the beam had been fastened to the floor. The axe had initially been held aloft by a cotton chord, attached to a hook that had been screwed into the wall. Below the chord was a small shelf on which a candle had been placed. When lit, the candle acted as a rudimentary timing device, burning firstly above the chord, but as it shortened it eventually reached the level of the chord, burning through it and releasing the axe to do its grizzly job.

A little bit of light detective work soon revealed that the device's inventor and victim were one and the same. So, who was the man and why did he go to such extraordinary lengths to top himself? His name was James A Moon and he was thirty-five years of age when he took his own life. A journalist writing for *The New York Times* on 15th June 1876 commented: 'Mr. Moon was well known in this city. He owned a fine farm near the Farmers' Institute, and leaves a wife and four children. He served with Capt. Haggard in the Sixteenth Indiana

Contemporary depiction of Karikari.

Battery during the war, and was a gallant soldier. Upon his farm he had a blacksmith, wagon, and a carpenter shop and was considered a mechanical genius.'

He had inherited a keen interest in all things mechanical from his father, but unfortunately he also inherited a propensity for suicide from his mother, who had killed herself some years earlier. He had attempted suicide twice before, firstly by trying to smother himself in a haystack, but he was discovered before the deed was done, and latterly by ingesting morphine, although in an insufficient quantity to kill him. Rather than relying on the notion of third time lucky, it seems Mr Moon decided to leave nothing to chance on the occasion he checked into the Lahr House.

On the preceding Friday, he had been to the local barber's shop to have his beard shaved off. From there, he visited a hardware store where he purchased the iron bars and from where he had purchased the axe some days previously. He also bought three ounces of chloroform. He then left home with a trunk containing everything he would need to construct his 'Karikari'. After assembling his killing machine, Moon strapped his legs to the floor and drew another strap across his chest, buckling it tight. The cotton wool in the box had been soaked with the chloroform, in order that once he placed his head inside, he would soon lose consciousness. He had precisely judged the trajectory of the axe blade and the purpose of the straps was to ensure he didn't move involuntarily in his unconscious state.

An article in the *Evansville Courier & Press*, a local newspaper, observed: 'The calculations were precise in every respect, and so completely was the head severed from the body that not a ligament was left to join it to the trunk. There can be no question but Moon wanted to demonstrate the utility of the machine, as well as to put an end to his own life, there is little doubt that he believed that someone would eventually patent "Karikari", and that his own memory, as the man who demonstrated its perfection, would be perpetuated by the act.'

The New York Times went even further, commenting: 'The appliances which had been used to produce death were most wonderful and will stand in the history of suicides without a parallel.' Ironically, however, it turns out that it was the ingenious device's precise purpose that would be its downfall. In response to a request for the likelihood of the patentability of the self-killing machine, the US Patent Office stated: 'Articles contrary to the public good are not patentable.' As suicide was illegal at the time, the patent that had apparently been applied for stood no chance of being granted. James A Moon, it transpired, would be the only person ever to make practical use of his 'Karikari'.

THIRTY-FIVE

THE RESURRECTION OF GEORGE HAYWARD

Before leaving the subject of death in Victorian times entirely behind, the following is an astonishing story that encompasses two of the era's greatest fears: namely, the dread of being buried alive and the scourge of grave robbers. The following account of Mr Hayward, sixty-nine, first appeared in *The Encyclopaedia of Death and Life in the Spirit-World* by John Reynolds Francis, published in 1900.

> "It was in Marshville, England, County Gloucestershire, where I was buried. I was quite young, and it was my chief delight to go to the fields with my older brothers… It was a bright morning when we started for the fields, and I ran ahead of the horses. The horses in England are not driven with reins, but they follow the command of the voice. After reaching the fields the pitching of the

straw commenced. The men used hop picks, which are fashioned somewhat after a heavy pitchfork. While standing near one of the hands, by accident I was struck on the head with one of the picks. It penetrated my scull (sic), and at the time, made me feel faint and dizzy. My injury was not considered serious. After returning to the house I was sent into the cellar, and much to my surprise, I could see in the dark as well as in the light. After coming from the cellar, my strength failed me, and I was soon bedfast.

Two doctors were called. One of them insisted that my condition was due to the blow on the head, the other that I had pleurisy. At any rate two weeks elapsed, and my eyes closed in supposed death. It was death as far as my relatives were concerned, yet I was painfully conscious of every movement going on around me. My eyes were half closed, and as I was laid out I heard my elder brother, John, walk into the house. I saw him approach the cot with tears in his eyes, and sympathizing friends consoled him by asking him to dry his tears. 'He is gone,' they said, and other similar expressions were used around the bier. Tears rained on my face as the burial shroud was wrapped around my body. As soon as the undertaker arrived, I knew I was to be buried alive. Try as I would, nothing could break the spell which bound me.

Well, the time for the funeral arrived, and the service was preached over my living but rigid body. The undertaker approached and the lid of my little prison-house was fastened down. Life seemed all but gone when this took place; but as I stated, no effort of mine could break the spell... I was painfully conscious of the fact that I was soon to be lowered into my grave. Strange as it may seem, at times I did not feel fear at my impending fate. The coffin was taken out of the wagon and lowered into the grave... The clods of earth fell heavy on the lid of the casket. There I was being entombed alive, unable to speak or stay the hands of my friends. My effort to move proved futile, and the close air of the coffin seemed stifling to me. Suddenly the shovelling ceased, and the silence of the tomb was complete. I did not seem to have the fear then that a person would naturally expect under such circumstances. All I remember is that the grave is a lonely place, and the silence of the tomb was horribly oppressive.

A dreamy sensation came over me, and a sense of suffocation became apparent. My whole system was paralysed; were it otherwise my struggles would have been desperate. How long I remained in this condition I do not know. The first sense of returning to life came over me when I heard the scraping of a spade on my coffin lid. I felt myself raised and borne away. I was taken out of my coffin, not to my home, but to a dissecting room. I beheld the doctors who had waited on me at my home, dressed in long white aprons. In their hands they had knives. Through my half closed eyes I saw them engaged in a dispute. They were trying to decide how to cut me up. One argued one way, while the other doctor took another view of the matter. All this I witnessed through my half open eyes. My sense of hearing was remarkably acute.

Both approached the table and opened my

Grave Robbers or Resurrectionists in Action.

mouth to take out my tongue, when, by superhuman effort, my eyelids were slightly raised. The next thing I heard was; 'Look out you fool, he is alive!' 'He is dead,' rejoined the other doctor. 'See, he opens his eyes!' continued the first doctor. The other physician let his knife drop, and a short time after that I commenced to recover rapidly. Instead of cutting me up, they took me home. There was great rejoicing among my relatives… I suppose I was kept alive for some purpose, for I am the father of ten children."

Unfortunately, George did not tell us what became of the doctors and their grave-robbing sidekicks. George

Hayward died for real in 1903, aged in his seventies. He is buried in Woodlawn Cemetery, Independence, Missouri, United States. What a remarkable story.

One note of caution. The place name of Marshville does not exist in Gloucestershire, England. There is, however, a Moreton-in-Marsh in Gloucestershire. Given that George was quite old when he recounted the tale and that he had clearly emigrated to the United States many years before, I am prepared to accept that he made a genuine mistake in his recollection of the place name.

THIRTY-SIX

THE ARTFUL DEXTER?

As an entrepreneur, Timothy Dexter was either extremely shrewd or extremely fortunate. Born in Malden, Massachusetts, Unites States on 22nd January 1747, his first acquisition was definitely shrewd, if somewhat unromantic. In 1769, aged just twenty-two, he married Elizabeth Frothingham, a wealthy widow ten years his senior, who owned her own house. However, his newly acquired wealth and comfortable home did not endear him to the upper echelons of local society, as he was relatively uneducated and somewhat eccentric. Consequently, he was shunned by the local business community, to such an extent that individuals would go out of their way to offer him bad advice, in the hope of bankrupting him.

However, this was not before Timothy experienced another lucky break or possibly exhibited a prudent approach to matters of finance, depending on which way you look at it. At the end of the American War of Independence, Dexter purchased large amounts of a virtually worthless currency, known as Continental currency, which had depleted so much during the conflict that it was regarded as valueless. At the end of the war, however, the US government made the decision to pay holders of the currency one per cent of its face value. Our young businessman had purchased so much of the stuff, that even one per cent of face value netted him enough profit on his investment to finance the building of two ships. Duly constructed and launched, he thus commenced an export business to the Caribbean and Europe.

Bed-warmers, which resembled a frying pan with a long handle and a lid, were popular household items in colder climates, before the advent of central heating. On the advice of one who wished him ill fortune, he took it upon himself to export a large quantity of bed-warmers to the West Indies – a region with a tropical climate. Once again, fortune was on his side. The captain of his ship, realising his overlord's error, marketed them locally as ladles to the molasses industry, which required just such items in the production process, and he was thus able to net his boss a considerable profit.

Another piece of bad advice upon which he acted was to ship coal to Newcastle, England. In the British Isles, the saying 'sending coals to Newcastle' means to send

Timothy Dexter.

something to somewhere it is not needed. The case in point being that Newcastle was, at that time, the largest coal-distribution centre in Britain. Once again, Timothy's luck was in, as his ship arrived at a time when miners were taking industrial action by striking, and so his cargo of coal sold for a premium rate.

On another occasion, he was advised to send a large consignment of woollen mittens to the Caribbean, where such items are not required due to the warm nature of the climate. However, as luck would have it, Asian merchants just happened to be in port when the consignment arrived and they duly bought the lot for export to Siberia, a part of the world where hands need to be kept warm. A similar shipment of gloves he sent to Polynesia was snapped up by Portuguese traders on their way to China.

Possibly out of jealousy resulting from his extraordinary good fortune, he was snubbed by his social contemporaries, most of whom regarded him as unintelligent and naive. Undeterred by his unpopularity, however, Dexter bought himself a much larger house in Newburyport, Massachusetts and proceeded to decorate it opulently, with minarets and a statue of a golden eagle.

More bizarrely, he commissioned forty wooden statues of famous men, which he placed around the grounds of the house. They included effigies of Thomas Jefferson, George Washington, William Pitt and Napoleon Bonaparte. He also commissioned a statue of himself, with a modest inscription that read: 'I am the fist in the East, the first in the West, and the greatest philosopher in the Western World'. He also oversaw the construction of his own mausoleum. It

Timothy Dexter's House.

was possibly around this time that he began to refer to himself as Lord Dexter – a title entirely of his own creation.

Another of his strange eccentricities concerned his wife, whom he told visitors had died, despite the fact that she was very much alive and still living in the house. Stunned guests were told that the woman they could see frequenting the property was actually her ghost.

Wondering how people will react to your death is something most of us will never know the answer to. Not so for Timothy Dexter, who faked his own death in order to find out. About 3000 people attended his fake wake, but he was not a happy man. Noting that his wife was not crying, Dexter revealed himself to the shocked gathering and promptly proceeded to beat her for not showing sufficient grief at her loss.

Not content with being a successful, if somewhat odd, businessman, Dexter next turned his attention to writing and, in 1802, published a book entitled, *A Pickle for the Knowing Ones*. In it, he berated politicians, the clergy and even his long-suffering wife. It was terrible. There was no punctuation and the spelling was unorthodox, to put it mildly. As an example, one section begins: 'Ime the first Lord in the younited States of A mercury Now of Newburyport it is the voise of the peopel and I cant Help it and so Let it goue'. It was so bad that it became popular for its novelty value and would eventually be reprinted eight times. Responding to criticism surrounding the lack of punctuation, the second edition contained an extra page purely made up of punctuation marks, which readers were instructed to insert wherever they liked.

Timothy Dexter died for real on 26th October 1806 aged fifty-nine, with his will including a bequest for the care of Newburyport's poor. His obituary contained the comment: 'his intellectual endowments not being of the most exalted stamp', which seems a little ungracious considering his final act of benevolence. The last word is, perhaps, best left to 19th-century author Sarah Anna Emery, who said of Dexter: 'Though ignorant and illiterate, and doubtless somewhat indebted to luck for his good fortune, still it is evident the man was both shrewd and sagacious.'

THIRTY-SEVEN

THE DISAPPEARANCE OF STAR DUST

On 2nd August 1947, a British South American Airways (BSAA) Avro Lancastrian airliner, named Star Dust, departed from Buenos Aires Airport, Argentina, at 1.46pm, bound for Santiago, Chile. At 5.41pm, the aircraft sent a message in Morse code to Santiago Airport, predicting an arrival time of 5.45pm. That time came and went without any sign of the BSAA flight. In fact, it never arrived. Despite extensive searches by both Argentine and Chilean search teams, and notwithstanding a five-day search operation directed by Air Vice Marshall Don Bennett, the head of BSAA, no trace of Star Dust, its passengers or crew could be found.

The Avro 691 Lancastrian 3 was a relatively new aircraft, having been first registered on 16th January 1946. It was capable of carrying up to thirteen passengers, although on the day in question only six passengers were on board, which, in addition to the crew of five, meant there were eleven individuals unaccounted for. The flight crew consisted of three experienced Royal Air Force pilots, namely Captain Reginald Cooke, forty-four; First Officer Norman Hilton Cooke, thirty-nine; and Second Officer Donald Checklin, twenty-seven. Radiotelegraph operator Dennis Harmer, twenty-seven, and flight attendant Iris Evans, twenty-six, made up the complement of five. The passengers consisted of five men of Palestinian, Swiss and British nationalities, including a United Kingdom diplomatic courier, and one female passenger, Marta Limpert – a German émigré.

To add further to the mystery, the last Morse code messages received from Star Dust were enigmatic, to say the least. The first of three messages was 'ETA SANTIAGO 17.45 HRS STENDEC'. As the radio operator at Santiago Airport did not recognise the last word of the transmission, he messaged back seeking clarification. In response, Star Dust's radiotelegraph operator repeated the word 'STENDEC' twice in quick succession, before contact with the aircraft was lost. Despite much speculation and proposed explanations, no definitive interpretation of 'STENDEC' has ever been established.

BSAA Lancastrian 3 G-AGWH Painted as Star Dust.

There are, however, theories. The three most plausible being as follows:

1. 'STENDEC' is an anagram of the word 'DESCENT', which is presumably what the airliner would have been doing at the time of the messages. Hypoxia is a condition caused by a lack of oxygen and symptoms include confusion and disorientation. Might the passengers and crew have been suffering from this condition, leading to the radiotelegraph operator inadvertently scrambling part of the message?
2. 'STENDEC' was an obscure abbreviation used by pilots with wartime experience meaning 'Severe Turbulence Encountered, Now Descending Emergency Crash-landing'. Although given the earlier part of the message, indicating an estimated arrival time at Santiago, this seems improbable.
3. The most compelling possible explanation, however, is that in Morse code 'STENDEC' uses the same dot-dash sequence as 'SCTI AR', but with different spacing between the characters, meaning a simple error in either the sending or receiving of the message could have been to blame. 'SCTI AR' is code and means 'Los Cerrillos Santiago, over'. An unabbreviated version of the message would therefore read as follows: 'Estimated time of arrival Santiago 17.45 hours, Los Cerrillos Santiago, over'.

So, what became of Star Dust? Absence of evidence led to many theories as to the fate of the aircraft and its occupants. These ranged from accident to sabotage and even to alien abduction by a UFO. However, in

1998, over fifty years after the disappearance of the airliner, two Argentinian mountaineers came upon a debris field that included the wreckage of a Rolls-Royce Merlin aircraft engine in the Tupungato Glacier at a height of 15,000 feet (4,600m), approximately 50 miles (80km) to the east of Santiago.

A subsequent expedition by the Argentine Army in 2000 discovered additional wreckage, which included wheels and a propeller. Sadly, but unsurprisingly, human remains were also recovered from the scene of the disaster. Accident investigators were able to make a number of deductions based on the remains of the aircraft, which led them in a certain direction. The wreckage was very localised and the condition of the propeller indicated that the engine had been running at close to cruising speed at the time of impact. Additionally, the condition of the wheels was very good, with one of the tyres being still inflated, indicating that the undercarriage was retracted at the time of the crash. All this pointed to a controlled flight into terrain, meaning it flew straight into the ground, as opposed to breaking up mid-air or attempting a crash-landing.

But if this is true, what caused an experienced flight crew to do such a thing? The answer, it seems, lay in a combination of environmental factors. In order to reach Santiago, Star Dust had to cross over the Andes mountain range at a height of 24,000 feet (7,300m), which necessitated the aircraft flying through the high altitude winds of the jet stream. In 1947, the effect of the jet stream was not fully appreciated and, on this occasion, the airliner would have encountered a significant headwind, considerably reducing its groundspeed – a factor of which the pilots were probably unaware. If we then add to the mix the heavy cloud cover through which the aircraft was flying, the crew would have had no visual points of reference with which to be able to make a judgement as to their precise location relative to the ground. They were essentially flying blind.

By failing to factor in the drag caused by the headwind of the jet stream, the pilots would likely have assumed a faster groundspeed and probably calculated that they had successfully crossed over the Andes mountains. Without ground vision due to the cloud cover, they seemingly did not realise that they were still flying over the mountain range and, as a consequence, in all likelihood, erroneously began their descent for Santiago too soon, flying headfirst into the side of Mount Tupungato, possibly without ever realising their mistake.

In all probability, Star Dust flew into a near-vertical snow field close to the top of the glacier. The resulting avalanche would have completely buried the wreckage within moments and concealed it from the contemporaneous search parties. In the ensuing years, the debris became incorporated into the glacier itself, with fragments gradually emerging farther down the mountain decades later, as a result of a combination of glacier movement and melting ice caused by climate change.

The human remains recovered were identified through DNA sampling. The remains of Captain Reginald Cooke finally returned home to Melbourne in Derbyshire, England, fifty-eight years after he left for work for the last time. He was laid to rest in his hometown in 2005.

THIRTY-EIGHT

THE REMARKABLE SURVIVAL OF EDWARD OXFORD

In approximately 2015, a man bought a house in the Canadian province of Quebec. Nothing remarkable about that, I agree, but it was what he discovered in an antique wooden chest, in a sealed-up section of the property's attic, that piqued the gentleman's interest. Inside were eighty-seven letters written by a man named Edward Allen Oxford to his wife, Mildred. It transpired that Edward was a lumberjack who, as a consequence of his profession, often spent extended periods of time away from home. Due to this enforced absence, Edward frequently wrote to Mildred, who, fortunately, kept his letters. The letters spanned a period from shortly after World War I until 1944, after which, it was presumed, he retired. It is understood the couple passed away within a short time of one another in the late 1940s.

As one might expect, the letters were affectionate and contained details about his life in the regional lumber camps in the forests of Canada. However, they also contained recollections of a remarkable occurrence that took place during World War I. It seemed that, on an unspecified date in 1916, Edward had been a merchant seaman on board an allied ship sailing off the coast of Antarctica, when it was torpedoed and sunk by a German U-boat. The location of the sinking was somewhere between Elephant Island and Deception Island, in the South Shetland archipelago. Conditions would have been harsh, to put it mildly. Indeed, it was shortly before this occurrence that Antarctic explorer Ernest Shackleton and his crew were forced to take shelter on Elephant Island after their ship, *The Endurance*, sank after having been crushed by pack ice in the Weddell Sea in November 1915. They survived in an upturned lifeboat on a diet of penguins and seals.

However, the experience of Edward Oxford appears to have been very different from that of Shackleton and his crew. Edward described being marooned for six weeks on a warm tropical island off

Contemporary image of a U-boat sinking a merchant ship.

the coast of Antarctica, with plentiful vegetation and wildlife for sustenance. Of course, no such island exists, or could have existed, in the frigid environment of the South Atlantic. A fanciful tale, dreamed up to impress the love of his life, you might imagine, except for a couple of things. Firstly, his recollections of the island were frequent and unwavering. His story was never contradictory and details never changed. Secondly, historical records support his unlikely story – sort of.

Imperial records confirm that Edward Allen Oxford had been a British merchant seaman who had been aboard a ship that was torpedoed in 1916, with the presumed loss of all cargo and crew. However, as we know, that is not the end of the story. Edward Oxford was eventually spotted by a passing ship and rescued. This is where things start to get, frankly, bizarre. He was spotted in 1918 standing on a tidal island. Yes, that's right, 1918 – a full two years after the sinking, not a mere six weeks as claimed by Oxford. So, what really happened, and how had he survived on an island that would have been submerged in freezing water for much of the day?

When questioned, he claimed that he had simply walked from the warm and tropical island on which he had been living since the sinking a mere six weeks ago to the island where he was spotted at low tide. The authorities decided that, owing to the impossibility of his story, he must have been suffering from some form of insanity and, accordingly, he was admitted to an appropriate facility in Nova Scotia in order for him to recover. It was there that he met a nurse by the name of Mildred Constance Landsmire. The two fell in love and after his release, they married and set up home together. Initially, Edward worked for a cousin on his nearby dairy farm. However, Edward soon decided that he was not suited to a life of agriculture and so turned his hand to the lumber industry, which is where he remained until retirement.

So, what are we to make of all this flummery? Well, unless we go back some ninety million years to when Antarctica was a thriving rainforest, it has, ever since, been a frigid environment, unsuitable for human survival, without the proper nutrients and equipment. A shipwrecked mariner in 1916 would be most unlikely to have had the requisite provisioning at his disposal. And yet there he stood, alone on an island that emerged from the icy waters for a few hours each day, seemingly in perfect health. His contemporaries could not explain the conundrum and so put his story down to the ramblings of a madman, leaving the question of what really happened to Edward unanswered.

Could he possibly have survived on a tidal island in freezing conditions, without food or shelter for two years? Of course not. Instead, might a number of the crew of the stricken vessel have escaped on a lifeboat, with enough warm clothing and provisions to sustain them for a period of time? Perhaps. But what then? There would not have been sufficient quantities of food and water to keep them going for two years. Might cannibalism have taken place as crew members eventually began to succumb to the harsh conditions? Possibly. If Oxford was the last man left and he spotted a rescue vessel, he may have had enough time to dispose of the evidence and all his life-sustaining equipment, while simultaneously concocting an elaborate story to cover the truth. However, this would have been very risky indeed. What if the ship failed to spot him and simply sailed away, leaving him to a frigid, watery fate? Overall, this scenario seems unlikely.

The other possibility is that something seemingly paranormal occurred. Quantum physicists study nature at atomic and subatomic levels, and have suggested the existence of multiple dimensions as distinctly possible. Might Edward have transgressed the dimensional veil and entered a parallel universe where Antarctica has a temperate climate, only slipping back again once rescue was at hand? Physicists also argue that although time appears linear to us, it isn't. Travelling through time should be as easy as moving through space, even though we don't seem to be able to accomplish the feat. Might Edward Oxford have become an inadvertent time traveller, transitioning back over millions of years and travelling back to the present in time for his rescue? In either of these scenarios, to have been removed from a perilous environment and returned only once salvation was at hand suggests his survival may have been at the hands of a higher authority.

Ultimately, a plausible explanation for the survival of Edward Allen Oxford does not readily present itself and, with over a century having passed since the events in question, one can only wonder. What a marvellously strange world we inhabit.

THIRTY-NINE

AND THE BAND PLAYED ON

On Friday 18th October 2013, a violin sold at an auction in Wiltshire, England for £900,000 ($1,457,000). It was not one of the famous Stradivarius instruments – in fact, it was not even a particularly high-quality violin, just an average old fiddle. Its condition also left much to be desired. The metalwork had rusted and the woodwork had suffered similarly. It was virtually unplayable. So, why was the knackered old thing so sought after and valuable? As you might guess, it has an intriguing back story.

To get to the beginning of the tale, let us start at the point of sale and work our way backwards. The purchaser of the violin chose to remain anonymous, though it was believed they were British. Although privately owned, the instrument is occasionally loaned out for display to museums around the world. At the time of writing, I am given to understand that it is on display in the United States. The vendor of the violin, who also chose to remain anonymous, had inherited it upon the death of his or her parents. The parent who possessed the instrument had learned to play the violin in the 1940s and had been gifted it by their music teacher. A letter from teacher to pupil referred to the present as being 'virtually unplayable, no doubt due to its eventful life'. The violin teacher had herself been given it by a Salvation Army bandmaster in whose band she played.

Shortly beforehand, the violin had been given to the Salvation Army, by a woman who had inherited it from her sister when she passed away in 1939. The deceased sister's name was Maria Robinson and the instrument had belonged to her fiancée, who had himself died several decades earlier. Upon the death of her betrothed, she had been given his violin as a keepsake. You will be pleased to know that we are now getting close to the reason for the instrument's value. The name of Maria's fiancée was Wallace Henry Hartley. Wallace Hartley had been the bandleader aboard RMS *Titanic*, who famously played on as the stricken vessel slipped beneath the waves on 15th April 1912, with the loss of over 1,500 lives. Sadly, Wallace was among those who died in the sinking. The violin in question is the very instrument Hartley had been playing as the disaster unfolded.

Now, I know what you're thinking. How did this instrument survive the sinking and not go down with the ship? And how do we know this is *that* violin? After all, with valuable antiques, provenance is everything. It is largely thanks to the painstaking efforts of one man, Alan Aldridge of auction house Henry Aldridge and Son, who spent seven years studying the instrument and tracing the trail back from the vendor all the way to Wallace Hartley himself, that we have the answers. Firstly, we have a paper trail in the form of two important documents. In the letter from the violin teacher to her pupil, she refers to the instrument's 'eventful life'. Further corroborating evidence came to light in the form of correspondence between Maria Robinson and the provincial secretary of Halifax, Nova Scotia, where the bodies recovered from the site of the sinking were brought. In it, she expresses her 'heartfelt thanks to all those concerned in the return of my late fiancée's violin'.

Wallace Hartley.

So how came the violin to be recovered? After all, the sombre task undertaken by the recovery vessels was the recovery of bodies, not musical instruments. The answer comes to us from contemporary newspaper articles, which reported the important information that when Wallace Hartley's body was recovered, it was found that he had strapped his music case about his person. The violin was contained therein. Apparently, he was very attached to that particular instrument and it seems he chose to enter the water with it strapped to his back in the hope of rescue, or possibly also as a means of identification in the event of death.

But perhaps the most compelling evidence is the instrument itself. Experts were engaged to study the violin with a view to establishing both its origin and the likelihood that it was the very instrument Hartley had been playing when the ship went down. Andrew Hooker, an expert on musical instruments, identified it as of German manufacture, and to it having been made between 1880 and 1900, making it of the right age. He also concluded that it would have been a mid-priced instrument at the time, which concurred with Hartley's requirements and status.

Additionally, forensic scientist Michael Jones carefully examined the violin and concluded that the corrosion to the metal was not only consistent with it having been immersed in seawater, but matched that of other metal objects recovered from the *Titanic*. A CT scan was also undertaken, which revealed that the glue used in its manufacture was of a type that would have been able to cope with both immersion in salt water and freezing temperatures. The scan also revealed two hairline cracks, which indicated that it had been subject to some degree of trauma. It is these cracks that rendered the instrument, for all intents and purposes, unplayable.

However, regardless of all the foregoing evidence, the most striking affirmation that this was Wallace Hartley's violin is also the most personal and poignant. A silver plaque attached to the tailpiece of the instrument reads: 'For Wallace On The Occasion of Our Engagement from Maria'. The plaque is hallmarked 1910, the year the couple became engaged, and expert analysis has concluded that it has been attached to the violin for a very long time.

A practising barrister was asked to examine the evidence and give his considered opinion as to the authenticity of the instrument. He concluded: 'The evidence presented does meet the standard of beyond reasonable doubt and is quite compelling'.

Amazingly, we even know the last tune played on the violin by Hartley as the ship went down. According to survivors, it was a very appropriate hymn, 'Nearer My God to Thee'. Wallace Henry Hartley's body was eventually returned to England. Hartley's father met the ship at Liverpool and brought his son's body back to his hometown of Colne, Lancashire. His funeral took place on 18th May 1912. One thousand people attended Hartley's funeral, while an estimated 30,000–40,000 lined the route of his funeral procession. Hartley's grave is in the Keighley Road Cemetery, Colne, where a 10-feet (3.0m) headstone, containing a carved violin at its base, was erected in his honour.

APPENDIX I

IMAGES

THE COMTE DE SAINT-GERMAIN: THE IMMORTAL COUNT?
The Comte de Saint-Germain. This work is in the public domain in its country of origin and other countries and areas where the copyright term is the author's life plus seventy years or less.
Richard Chanfray. This file is licensed under the Creative Commons Attribution-Share Alike 4.0 International license.

BEAR NECESSITIES
A Contemporary Illustration of the Attack – Unknown. This media file is in the public domain in the United States. This applies to US works where the copyright has expired, often because its first publication occurred prior to 1st January 1923.
Hugh Glass Monument – John Lopez. This file is licensed under the Creative Commons Attribution-Share Alike 4.0 International license.

THE REMARKABLE LIFE AND TIMES OF CHARLES HERBERT LIGHTOLLER
Charles Lightoller (circa 1910). This UK artistic work, of

which the author is unknown and cannot be ascertained by reasonable enquiry, is in the public domain.
A Depiction of the Titanic Disaster – Willy Stöwer. The author died in 1931, so this work is in the public domain in its country of origin and other countries and areas where the copyright term is the author's life plus eighty years or less.
Charles' Boat, *Sundowner*. Dunkirk Little Ship Sundowner in Ramsgate Harbour, Ramsgate, Kent. Stavros1. This file is licensed under the Creative Commons Attribution 3.0 Unported license.

THE REMARKABLE LIFE OF SIR ARTHUR CONAN DOYLE
Sir Arthur Conan Doyle in 1914. The author died in 1942, so this work is in the public domain in its country of origin and other countries and areas where the copyright term is the author's life plus eighty years or less.

THE ENIGMATIC DB COOPER
Artist's Impression of DB Cooper. This image is a work of a United States Department of Justice employee, taken or made as part of that person's official duties. As a work of the US federal government, the image is in the public domain
Boeing 727 With Lowered Rear Staircase. This file is licensed under the Creative Commons Attribution-Share Alike 3.0 Unported license.

THE DISAPPEARANCE OF FREDERICK VALENTICH
Frederick Valentich. This image or other work is of Australian origin and is now in the public domain because its term of copyright has expired.
A Cessna 182. This file is made available under the Creative Commons CC0 1.0 Universal Public Domain Dedication.

GOD'S OWN DIVER
Winchester Cathedral. WyrdLight.com. This file is licensed under the Creative Commons Attribution 3.0 Unported license.

West Window. Gill Hicks: Stained Glass Window, Winchester Cathedral / CC BY-SA 2.0.
William Walker – John Crook. This work is in the public domain in its country of origin and other countries and areas where the copyright term is the author's life plus seventy years or less.
Bust of William Walker at Winchester Cathedral – *Jan Kamenícek*. William Walker statuette at Winchester Cathedral, England. I, the copyright holder of this work, release this work into the public domain. This applies worldwide.

THE GHOST WHO SOLVED HIS OWN MURDER?
Maria Talarico. This image is in the public domain because the copyright of this photograph has expired.

THE EXTENDABLE CLARENCE WILLARD
A Double Negative Photograph of Clarence Willard Demonstrating His Remarkable Ability. This work is in the public domain because it was published in the United States between 1928 and 1977, inclusive, without a copyright notice.

TITANIC TWICE?
Morgan Robertson (1861–1915) – taken by George G. Rockwood between 1890 and 1900. This work is in the public domain in its country of origin and other countries and areas where the copyright term is the author's life plus seventy years or less.
An Artist's Impression of the Sinking of the *Titanic* – Willy Stöwer, 1912. The author died in 1931, so this work is in the public domain in its country of origin and other countries and areas where the copyright term is the author's life plus eighty years or less.

COLONEL BLOOD AND THE CROWN JEWELS HEIST
Colonel(?) Thomas Blood, 1813. This media file is in the public domain.
A Depiction of the Scene of Crime, 1793. Blood and

His Accomplices Making their Escape after Stealing the Crown of Charles the Second in The Jewel House by George Younghusband (1921). This work is in the public domain in its country of origin and other countries and areas where the copyright term is the author's life plus one hundred years or less.
King Charles II with his Crown – Peter Lely. Portrait of King Charles II (1630–1685) by Peter Lely (1618–1680) Charles II is portrayed wearing the robes of the Sovereign of the Order of the Garter. This work is in the public domain in its country of origin and other countries and areas where the copyright term is the author's life plus one hundred years or less.

THE ELECTRIFYING ANDREW CROSSE
Andrew Crosse (1784–1855) – unknown artist. This work is in the public domain in its country of origin and other countries and areas where the copyright term is the author's life plus seventy years or less.
An Example of the Genus Acarus – Acarologiste, own work. This file is licensed under the Creative Commons Attribution-Share Alike 4.0 International license.

HELL ON EARTH
Centralia Before and After the Demolition of Properties. This file is licensed under the Creative Commons Attribution-Share Alike 2.0 Generic license.

THE CURSE OF FLIGHT 191
American Airlines McDonnell Douglas DC-10. This work is free and may be used by anyone for any purpose. If you wish to use this content, you do not need to request permission.

THE STRANGE CASE OF THE ACTRESS AND THE SKELETON
Ada Constance Kent. No known copyright restrictions.

THE REAL EBENEZER SCROOGE
John Elwes (1714–1789). This work is in the public domain in its country of origin and other countries and

areas where the copyright term is the author's life plus one hundred years or less.
Jemmy Wood (1756–1836). This work is in the public domain in its country of origin and other countries and areas where the copyright term is the author's life plus seventy years or less.

TAMAM SHUD – THE SOMERTON MAN MYSTERY
Somerton Man. This file is in the public domain because this photo was taken in 1948 and is out of copyright under Australian law.
Somerton Man Headstone. This work has been released into the public domain by its author.

A DEGREE OF ERROR
Douglas Corrigan Standing next to His Aircraft. This image or file is a work of a US Air Force Airman or employee, taken or made as part of that person's official duties. As a work of the US federal government, the image or file is in the public domain.

ABANDONED CYPRUS
Varosha As It Is Today. This file is licensed under the Creative Commons Attribution-Share Alike 4.0 International license.
Abandoned Passenger Terminal. This file is licensed under the Creative Commons Attribution-Share Alike 3.0 Unported license.
Still Awaiting Departure. This file is licensed under the Creative Commons Attribution-Share Alike 3.0 Unported license.

HOORAY HENRY
Henry Cyril Paget, 5th Marquess of Anglesey. This work is in the public domain in its country of origin and other countries and areas where the copyright term is the author's life plus seventy years or less.

THE MYSTERIOUS DEATH OF ALFRED LOEWENSTEIN
Alfred Loewenstein. Public domain.

IMAGES

KORLA PANDIT, THE INDIAN MUSIC MAESTRO?
Korla Pandit. It is believed that the use of images of promotional material to illustrate where the image is unrepeatable, i.e. a free image could not be created to replace it, qualifies as fair use under Copyright law.

THE MANY LIVES OF STANLEY JACOB WEINBERG
Weinberg, on the Left, During the Visit of Princess Fatima to the White House. Library of Congress. No known restrictions on publication.

BITTERSWEET KISS
Dead Man Riding. This work is in the public domain in the United States because it was published (or registered with the US Copyright Office) before 1st January 1928.

A STRANGE ROMANCE
Carl Tanzler in 1940. This file is licensed under the Creative Commons Attribution 2.0 Generic license.
Maria Elena Milagro de Hoyos in Life and Death. This file is licensed under the Creative Commons Attribution 2.0 Generic license.

THE MEN FROM NOWHERE
Andorra is Indeed Located Between France and Spain. This file is licensed under the Creative Commons Attribution-Share Alike 3.0 Unported license.

THE MYSTERIOUS DEATH OF ELISA LAM AT THE CECIL HOTEL
Elizabeth Short. This work is in the public domain in the United States because it was published in the United States between 1928 and 1977, inclusive, without a copyright notice.

PORKY BICKAR AND THE MOUNT EDGECUMBE ERUPTION
The Eruption of Mount Edgecumbe – Harold Wahlman, 1st April 1974. Wahlman was walking across the Alice Island footbridge when he noticed smoke rising from

Mount Edgecumbe, so he ran home to get his camera. No known copyright restrictions.

Porky Bickar. Porky Bickar in 1991. Courtesy of the Daily Sitka Sentinel.

THE SCIENCE OF LAZARUS
Doctor Robert E Cornish. This work is in the public domain because it was published in the United States between 1928 and 1963, and although there may or may not have been a copyright notice, the copyright was not renewed.

THE WHIMSICAL HORACE DE VERE COLE
Horace de Vere Cole. This work is in the public domain in its country of origin and other countries and areas where the copyright term is the author's life plus seventy years or less.
The Dreadnought Hoaxers. This work is in the public domain in its country of origin and other countries and areas where the copyright term is the author's life plus seventy years or less.

JACOB MILLER'S TOUGH NUT
Jacob Miller in His Later Years. This work is in the public domain because it was published (or registered with the US Copyright Office) before 1st January 1928.

THE SIN-EATERS
Sin-Eating. No known copyright restrictions.
The Grave of Richard Munslow. No known copyright restrictions.

THE AMAZING VICTORIAN MACHINE OF DEATH
A Contemporary Depiction of Karikari. No known copyright restrictions.

THE RESURRECTION OF GEORGE HAYWARD
Grave Robbers or Resurrectionists in Action. This work is in the public domain in its country of origin and other countries and areas where the copyright term is the author's life plus one hundred years or less.

THE ARTFUL DEXTER?
Timothy Dexter. This work is in the public domain in its country of origin and other countries and areas where the copyright term is the author's life plus seventy years or less. **Timothy Dexter's House.** This media file is in the public domain. This applies to works where the copyright has expired, often because its first publication occurred prior to 1st January 1928, and if not then due to lack of notice or renewal.

THE DISAPPEARANCE OF STAR DUST
BSAA Lancastrian 3 G-AGWH Painted as Star Dust. This image is a photograph from San Diego Air & Space Museum at Flickr Commons. According to the museum, there are no known restrictions on the publication of these photos.

THE REMARKABLE SURVIVAL OF EDWARD OXFORD
Contemporary Image of a U-boat Sinking a Merchant Ship. The author died in 1931, so this work is in the public domain in its country of origin and other countries and areas where the copyright term is the author's life plus eighty years or less.

AND THE BAND PLAYED ON
Wallace Hartley. This work was published before 1st January 1913 and it is anonymous or pseudonymous due to unknown authorship. It is in the public domain in the United States as well as countries and areas where the copyright terms of anonymous or pseudonymous works are 110 years or fewer since publication.

Appendix 2

SOURCES

The Comte de Saint-Germain: The Immortal Count?
www.liveabout.com/Saint-Germain-the-immortal-count-2594421
en.wikipedia.org/wiki/Count_of_St._Germain

Bear Necessities
www.lflank.wordpress.com/2015/02/14/think-youre-tough-the-story-of-hugh-glass
en.wikipedia.org/wiki/Hugh_Glass

The Remarkable Life and Times of Charles Herbert Lightoller
www.allthatsinteresting.com/charles-lightoller
en.wikipedia.org/wiki/Charles_Lightoller

The Strange Double Life of Emilie Sagee
www.timesofindia.indiatimes.com/readersblog/james/emilie-sagee-and-the-strange-case-of-the-doppelganger-5362
www.theconfessionalspodcast.com/the-blog/5-historical-figures-who-saw-their-doppelganger-and-then-died

The Remarkable Life of Sir Arthur Conan Doyle
Britannica.com
Wikipedia.org

SOURCES

The Enigmatic DB Cooper
www.britannica.com/biography/D-B-Cooper
en.wikipedia.org/wiki/D._B._Cooper
History's Greatest Mysteries, 2020

The Disappearance of Fredrick Valentich
skepticalinquirer.org/2013/11/the-valentich-disappearance-another-ufo-cold-case-solved
en.wikipedia.org/wiki/Disappearance_of_Frederick_Valentich

God's Own Diver
www.winchester-cathedral.org.uk/explore/famous-people
en.wikipedia.org/wiki/Winchester_Cathedral
en.wikipedia.org/wiki/William_Walker_(diver)

The Ghost Who Solved His Own Murder?
mysteriousuniverse.org
realitypod.com

The Extendable Clarence Willard
weirdhistorian.com
en.wikipedia.org/wiki/Clarence_E._Willard

Titanic Twice?
en.wikipedia.org/wiki/The_Wreck_of_the_Titan:_Or,_Futility
en.wikipedia.org/wiki/Morgan_Robertson

Colonel Blood and the Crown Jewels Heist
en.wikipedia.org/wiki/Jewel_House
en.wikipedia.org/wiki/Crown_Jewels_of_the_United_Kingdom
en.wikipedia.org/wiki/Thomas_Blood
www.bankofengland.co.uk/monetary-policy/inflation/inflation-calculator

The Electrifying Andrew Crosse
www.historicmysteries.com/andrew-crosse-experiment
en.wikipedia.org/wiki/Andrew_Crosse

Hell on Earth
www.rare.us/rare-life/centralia-mine-fire-pa-burning
en.wikipedia.org/wiki/Centralia_mine_fire

The Curse of Flight 191
Wikipedia.org

The Strange Case of the Actress and the Skeleton
mysteriousuniverse.org
coolinterestingstuff.com

The Real Ebeneezer Scrooge
en.wikipedia.org/wiki/Ebenezer_Scrooge
en.wikipedia.org/wiki/John_Elwes_(politician)
en.wikipedia.org/wiki/Jemmy_Wood

Tamam Shud – The Somerton Man Mystery
www.allthatsinteresting.com/tamam-shud-somerton-man
en.wikipedia.org/wiki/Tamam_Shud_case

A Degree of Error
en.wikipedia.org/wiki/Douglas_Corrigan
en.wikipedia.org/wiki/Charles_Lindbergh

Abandoned Cyprus
www.coolinterestingstuff.com/abandoned-Nicosia-international-airport
www.coolinterestingstuff.com/Varosha-the-abandoned-resort
en.wikipedia.org/wiki/Cyprus
en.wikipedia.org/wiki/Varosha,_Famagusta
en.wikipedia.org/wiki/Nicosia_International_Airport
Stavroula Michael

Hooray Henry
www.dailypost.co.uk/whats-on/5th-marquess-anglesey-life-history-14012663
en.wikipedia.org/wiki/Henry_Paget,_5th_Marquess_of_Anglesey

The Mysterious Death of Alfred Loewenstein
www.coolinterestingstuff.com/the-strange-mystery-of-alfred-Loewenstein
en.wikipedia.org/wiki/Alfred_Loewenstein
Fuller, John G, The Airmen Who Would Not Die (G.P. Putnam's Sons: New York, 1979)

SOURCES

Korla Pandit – The Indian Music Maestro
www.messynessychic.com/2019/07/11/the-tale-of-hollywoods-most-curious-career-imposter
en.wikipedia.org/wiki/Korla_Pandit

The Many Lives of Stanley Jacob Weinberg
www.atlasobscura.com/articles/imposter-brooklyn-weyman-clifford
en.wikipedia.org/wiki/Stanley_Clifford_Weyman

Bittersweet Kiss
www.headstuff.org/culture/history/1900-present/flogging-dead-jockey-frank-hayes
en.wikipedia.org/wiki/Frank_Hayes_(jockey)

A Strange Romance
www.coolinterestingstuff.com
en.wikipedia.org/wiki/Carl_Tanzler

The Men From Nowhere
www.ancient-origins.net
www.coolinterestingstuff.com/the-strange-mystery-of-the-man-from-taured
coolinterestingstuff.com/the-strange-mystery-of-jophar-vorin

The Mysterious Death of Elisa Lam at the Cecil Hotel
www.coolinterestingstuff.com/the-mysterious-case-of-elisa-lam
en.wikipedia.org/wiki/Cecil_Hotel_(Los_Angeles)
www.youtube.com/watch?v=MzptaoR5di0

Porky Bickar and the Mount Edgecumbe Eruption
hoaxes.org/af_database/permalink/the_eruption_of_mount_edgecumbe
en.wikipedia.org/wiki/Mount_Edgecumbe_(Alaska)

The Science of Lazarus
alphahistory.com
mysteriousuniverse.org
wikipedia.org

The Whimsical Horace de Vere Cole
https://en.wikipedia.org/wiki/Horace_de_Vere_Cole
www.thevintagenews.com/2019/04/20/Horace-de-vere-Cole

Jacob Miller's Tough Nut
medium.com
wearethemighty.com

The Sin-Eaters
www.weirdhistorian.com/the-funeral-rite-few-could-stomach
en.wikipedia.org/wiki/Sin-eater
www.findagrave.com/memorial/58880934/richard-munslow

The Amazing Victorian Machine of Death
Woodyard, C, The Victorian Book of the Dead (Kestrel Publications: 2014)

The Resurrection of George Hayward
Woodyard, C, The Victorian Book of the Dead (Kestrel Publications: 2014)

The Artful Dexter?
www.newenglandhistoricalsociety.com/
en.wikipedia.org

The Disappearance of Star Dust
www.theguardian.com
www.wikipedia.org
www.dailymail.co.uk

The Remarkable Survival of Edward Oxford
www.medium.com
www.popularmechanics.com

And the Band Played On
www.bbc.co.uk/news/england/wiltshire
www.encyclopedia-titanica.org
www.wikipedia.org